THE

INDIANA SCHOOLS

AND THE

Men who have worked in them.

EDITED BY

JAS. H. SMART, A. M.

STATE SUPERINTENDENT OF PUBLIC INSTRUCTION

PUBLISHED FOR THE COMMITTEE

BY

WILSON, HINKLE & CO.

CINCINNATI

Committee

JAMES H. SMART
ALEXANDER M. GOW
GEORGE P. BROWN
WILLIAM A. BELL

ELECTROTYPED AT
FRANKLIN TYPE FOUNDRY
CINCINNATI

ECLECTIC PRESS
WILSON, HINKLE & CO.
CINCINNATI

NOTE.

AT a meeting of the State Board of Education, held at Indianapolis, April 27, 1875, a committee, consisting of JAS. H. SMART, ALEX. M. GOW, GEO. P. BROWN, and WM. A. BELL, was appointed to prepare and supervise an exhibit of the educational products of the State at the International Exposition at Philadelphia in 1876. At a meeting of the committee held in July, 1875, it was resolved to publish a history of educational effort in the State, and Jas. H. Smart was directed to solicit contributions therefor, and to arrange the same for the press.

TABLE OF CONTENTS.

CHAPTER VI.

CHAPTER VII.

CHAPTER VIII.

CHAPTER IX.

EARLY SCHOOL DAYS.

BY

BARNABAS C. HOBBS, LL.D.

EARLY SCHOOL DAYS.

INTRODUCTION.—Being one year older than my native State, I have witnessed its rapid transition from a wilderness, mainly inhabited by savages, to a rank in civilization and intelligence surpassed by but few of her sister states.

While Indiana is the twenty-fourth State in area, she is first in her invested school fund, which amounts to $8,799,191; the fifth in population and in the number of her schools; the sixth in churches; the seventh in wealth; and the twenty-second in bonded indebtedness. These items may be taken as the best index of the character of her people.

I have seen the old-fashioned teacher behind his desk in true "Ichabod" style, just as he came across the ocean, who taught reading, writing, and ciphering as the full common school curriculum.

I have witnessed the neighborhood sensations when English grammar, geography, history, and philosophy, were introduced. I have watched the progress of education year by year, as broader and fuller culture, better "methods of instruction," and greater "professional ability" have been demanded, and have seen many teachers disappear from the professional ranks who could not, or would not, keep up with the age. Our work has been mainly one of self-development. Whilst we have profited much by the example of other states, our people have acquired strength, wealth, and intelligence by incentives and means which they themselves have originated. Our soil, heavy forests, and rich mineral resources, have conspired to draw hither an enterprising and intelligent population: a grand future awaits us.

The Pioneer School Buildings.—Pleasing reminiscences come before me when I think of the pioneer school-houses. They were made of hewed logs, and had puncheon floors and capacious chimneys and fireplaces. They had also seats without backs, and two long pins above the teacher's desk, on which his whips were laid.

The State then had no school revenue to distribute, and its school laws were mainly a method for selling school lands, for house building, choosing teachers, etc. Each voter was made a builder. By common consent the voters divided themselves into choppers, hewers, carpenters, masons, etc. If any could not report for duty, they might pay an equivalent for work in nails, glass, boards, or other material which could be used in building. If they neither worked nor paid an equivalent, they could be fined 37½ cents per day.

When completed, the building was inspected by the Township Trustees. If unsatisfactory, the workmen were again summoned and the work completed as desired, when a school could be taught in it by authority of the State.

The following quotations from the school law of 1824 will give a comprehensive outline of the educational work of that day, and will show the privations and disadvantages met with in inaugurating our present system of public schools, which has been so abundantly crowned with success.

SCHOOL LAW OF 1824 FOR BUILDING, ETC.—Sec. 6. Each "able-bodied male person of the age of twenty-one or upwards, being a freeholder or householder residing in the school district, shall be liable equally to work one day in each week until such building may be completed, or pay the sum of thirty-seven and one-half cents for every day he may so fail to work * * * * and provided, moreover, that the said Trustees shall always be bound to receive at cash price, in lieu of any such labor or money as aforesaid, any plank, nails, glass, or other materials which may be needed about said building."

Sec. 7. "That in all cases such school-house shall be eight feet between the floors, and at least one foot from the surface of the ground to the first floor, and finished in a manner calculated to render comfortable the teacher and pupils, with a suitable number of seats, tables, lights, and every thing necessary for the convenience of such school, *which shall be forever open for the education of all children within the district without distinction.*"

Section ten provided that, when finished, the house should be examined by Trustees, numbered, and named, and that subsequent needful repairs should be made.

HOW SCHOOLS WERE ORGANIZED.—As soon as the house was in readiness, the inhabitants were called together by the Trustees, at such school-house, to determine whether they would have any tax raised either by money or produce, to support a school, and what time the school should continue. If any part of the tax was to be in money, the proportion was determined, and a report was made to the Township Trustees, who kept the record of their proceedings, attended to collections, and, if needful, brought suit against delinquents.

The above duties having been performed, the District Trustees selected a teacher, and they, being required by law to employ him on "the most advantageous terms," entered in the contract, or "Article of Agreement," what produce would be paid him and where it should be delivered, and what part of the payment should be made in money; said "Article" also stated whether he would "board round" among the employers or not. A copy of said contract was required to go upon the record of the Township Trustees.

The Trustees were required to examine teachers before they could enter upon duty "touching their qualifications, and particularly as respects their knowledge of the English language, writing, and arithmetic." They were required also to certify whether, in their opinion, the applicants would be useful persons to be employed as teachers in said schools.

In 1837 a very important revision of the school law was made. The new law required that three County Examiners should be chosen to relieve the Township Trustees of the onerous and important duty of examining teachers. This was a new era in our educational system. The State had been wise and sagacious enough that year to appropriate to the school funds the $860,254 apportioned to Indiana in the national distribution of the public revenue. The public schools now became an object of much interest to the State, and teachers entered upon their work with county instead of township honors. I shall not forget my first experience under the new system. The only question asked me at my first examination was, "What is the product of 25 cents by 25 cents?" We had then no Teachers' Institutes, Normal Schools, nor "best methods" by which nice matters were determined and precise definitions given. We were not as exact then as people are now. We had only Pike's Arithmetic, which gave the "sums" and the rules. These were considered enough at that day. How could I tell the product of 25 cents by 25 cents, when such a problem could not be found in the book? The examiner thought it was 6¼ cents, but was not sure. I thought just as he did, but this looked too small to both of us. We discussed its merits for an hour or more, when he decided that he was sure I was qualified to teach school, and a first-class certificate was given me. How others fared, I can not tell. I only know that teachers rarely taught twice at the same place. Occasionally we had a man of merit, who continued several successive terms. Successful teachers were almost sure to become doctors or lawyers, or else to engage in some more lucrative employment.

WHENCE CAME THEY?—The pioneer teachers were generally adventurers from the East, or from England, Scotland, or Ireland, who sought temporary employment during winter while waiting for an "opening for business." Some of these were first-class men, and left a lasting good impression. One I remember well. His name was Albert Banks, and he came from Massachusetts. From him I learned my first lessons in English grammar. His career was short. The next summer, moving to a malarious district, he died of fever, lamented by all who knew him. His widow is now the estimable wife of Walter Benton, of Brownstown, in Jackson County.

Another class were men unsuccessful in trade, or who were lame or otherwise disabled. I once went to school to a retired liquor seller, who was very corpulent, and sedentary in his habits. He was extraordinarily faithful in beginning early and "keeping" late. School commenced at seven in summer, and seven and a half in winter. Recesses, morning and afternoon, were five minutes long, and we had one hour at noon. We were fully ten hours in school in summer. How scarcely endurable was that confinement! We had to sit on backless benches all those long days, and we wished—anxiously wished, recess or noon or night would come. Hours seemed like ages. May no generation ever be so punished again. But there was some silver lining to that cloud in my early school days. It is unreasonable to suppose that two hundred and fifty pounds avoirdupois could sit in one corner of any house all day without getting sleepy. Peace to his memory. When the naps came there was relief to the school. We ever enjoyed these genial occasions, and dreaded to see the gentleman wake up. I never complained of his needed siestas.

He was an easy, good-natured teacher. He could chew tobacco all day, and he generally kept about one yard square on the wall beside him damp. He was very accommodating to work my hard "sums" in long division and to rub them out dry so that it was no trouble to copy them. He made a rule that whoever came to school first in the morning, should take the head of his class all day. I had succeeded a few times in getting to school first, when the contest became spirited. I was there one morning in winter before five o'clock, with lunch for breakfast, and found a tall, young fellow there who had never before shown any interest in being first. What could it mean? Soon another like him came; and then another and another, until six or eight were there, whispering and acting mysteriously. I could not have been more than twelve years old. About sunrise the teacher came. The club went out to meet him. It was soon currently reported that they were to have a gallon of liquor for Christmas. We had an unusually quiet day. I never tried to be first any more at that school. The rule went down. I think that treat was the last in that district. The custom became unpopular there, though kept up many years in other places.

THE FIRST LADY TEACHER.—A very accomplished lady teacher from a bright center in North Carolina, taught a summer school in southern Indiana in the early day. Many had doubts about her success. It was not considered possible for a woman to govern a school. She had read much and could talk well. She had a happy way of illustrating prose and poetry by anecdotes of history and biography, and she could tell much about mythology. The lessons of poetry in Murray's Introduction and English Reader became intensely interesting after her stories about Greece and Rome, Ajax, Pegasus, and Parnassus. She stirred within me a love for classic literature, history, and art, which has never abated, and which has led me to buy many books that would not otherwise have been bought. She lived a few years, imperfectly appreciated, and went to the upper Kingdom. The question was settled that a lady could teach school as well as a gentleman. Woman's influence, culture, and adaptation to the educational work of the State has now become so well appreciated that one-half of the teachers of the State are females. Morally, intellectually, and socially she is shaping the character of the present generation, and is giving inspiration to those who will soon be intrusted with church and state. May our sons grow up, under her genial influence, as plants in their youth, and our daughters be polished after the similitude of a palace. Woman's happiness is only made secure where peace, intelligence, and virtue dwell.

We had once in southern Indiana a bachelor Irishman, rather gentlemanly in his personal appearance, who was above mediocrity as a teacher. He was very strong in his partialities and antipathies. When he had a favorite he petted and blarneyed him; but when he took a dislike to girl or boy, doomsday soon came. He was terrible when his wrath was kindled. The good and the bad in him were so well balanced that all disliked and dreaded him; he was too good to be set aside. He taught penmanship and arithmetic to perfection. It was not unusual for some of his scholars to "go through arithmetic," and to work the fractions without skipping them. This was the highest standard of scholarship in the rural districts of that day.

We had another teacher from the East, a lame man. He taught penmanship well, and this was the center and circumference of his circle of sciences. The clearest recollection I have of him now, has reference to the difficult times he had in poising fallen chunks on the poker in order to toss them back upon the huge fire. When he thought he had them well balanced, and attempted to send them up, they would whirl to one side and fall back, producing great merriment among the children, who were intently watching these experiments, and who would instinctively laugh at his failures. On discovering our indiscretion and impoliteness, it was no unusual thing for him to whip twelve or twenty of us in rapid succession until his wrath was appeased and his honor vindicated.

MORALITY IN SCHOOL.—By the penal laws of 1824, a fine of from one to three dollars was imposed for "vending or using playing-cards;" for "sporting, rioting, quarreling, hunting, fishing, or for common labor on the Sabbath." Every person of the age of fourteen or above, who would "profanely curse or damn, or profanely swear by the name of God, Jesus Christ, or the Holy Ghost," was fined for each offense from one to three dollars, but not more than ten dollars in one day. Like fines were also imposed for "playing bullets, for puppet shows, wire-dancing and tumbling, for money or reward."

The pioneers were eminently a religious people. They were high-toned and patriotic, and had great regard for law and order. It was not safe for any man to swear profanely when in the presence of any authority that could impose a fine. Men had to obey for wrath, if not for conscience. There was a strong repugnance to immorality generally, however much the people might have been deficient in general culture or learning. They were intensely but sincerely sectarian in their religious views, and this feeling would often crop out in school. Whatever might have been their religious differences, they agreed well in requiring children, at home and at school, to cultivate good habits and polite manners, to avoid profanity and all immoral and vulgar language or conduct; and the teacher was censured if he did not punish offenses deservedly; and if complaint was made at home because of such penalties, the result was a duplicate by the parents.

It was the age of brave men, being soon after the war of 1812. Though religious they were men of honor, and ever held themselves in readiness to vindicate their honor by hard knocks when they thought it necessary. This principle was strongly inculcated in the minds of their children, and it was no unusual thing to have a fight at school. It was generally very difficult, on such occasions, to find the merits of the fracas for want of correct testimony, or to determine exactly which was the innocent party. Often both combatants were whipped, that the scales of justice might be made to balance.

Their Religion a Good Educator.—Their religious teachers far excelled those of the present day in one particular. They were eminently successful in training their congregations to patient endurance and continued attention. The ability of the preacher was largely measured by the length of his sermons, which were from one to three hours long. They brought their ideals from Scotland and England. The modern American system had not then been introduced. A man's reputation would have been jeopardized who would have dared to criticize a three-hour sermon. He would have been esteemed inferior in judgment, piety, and Christian appreciation. Now any body can say what he pleases about preachers, and almost any audience is sated to repletion in forty or fifty minutes, however important the subject or attractive the manner.

THEIR SCHOOL GOVERNMENT AN ABSOLUTE MONARCHY.—When a school-house was built in the olden time, one of its indispensable appendages was two wooden pins, as before stated, over the teacher's desk, on which the whips could be laid. These were generally well-trimmed beech or hazel rods, from two to six feet in length. Sometimes the teacher would have half a dozen in readiness—some well worn, and others kept in reserve. Teachers were expected to govern on the home plan. The Christian people of that day had great faith in the wisdom of Solomon, who has left an aphorism for family government: "He that spareth his rod, hateth his son."

They believed the rod had a twofold virtue. It was not only a terror to evil-doers, but was a specific against stupidity and idleness. It was used as freely on the boy or girl who failed to recite well, as on him who was guilty of a misdemeanor. It so happened that some excellent men and women were brought up under this *regime*. Beech and hazel rods had a wonderfully stirring effect on both mind and body. The moral law favors an appeal to wrath as well as to conscience; and I am not sure but "Young America" would be a better boy to-day if he had more "bitter herbs" in his cup of joy.

Somehow the rod has become very unpopular in school. The old system made it merit a bad name. Our "improved methods" now exclude it—the effect, no doubt, of too great reaction from its extreme use in other days. It properly belongs to the lower story of humanity, but unfortunately that story has the most inhabitants.

Many pioneer teachers prided themselves on their masterly ability to govern, and kept ferule or rod constantly in their hand, as well as a goose-quill pen behind their ear. I have studied many a lesson in the consciousness that a failure was sure to receive a stinging reward. The fault of the system of that day was that conscience was not sufficiently regarded as the greatest, highest, and most desirable restraint on the one hand, and the surest incentive to duty on the other. The rod should come into use only when conscience is dormant.

LOUD SCHOOLS.—In the pioneer period, loud schools were in universal esteem. All our work was noisy; but when the hour came for learning the spelling lesson, never was so grand a concert. Sound intensified the memory, and gave a wonderful inspiration. How children like sound! If music is "the harmony of discord," we had it. This system was not without its merits. Boys and girls were educated to think in the midst of such surroundings. A celebrated Scotch teacher, Alexander Kinmont, of Cincinnati, as late as 1837, would conduct a school by no other method. He claimed that it is the practical philosophic system, by which boys can be trained for business on a steamboat wharf or any other place! Silent schools, however, in time supplanted the noisy ones, but many were very sure the old method was the best.

METHODS OF INSTRUCTION.—1. *Penmanship.* A good penman was held in great esteem, and much time and attention were given to writing. It was made a tedious and painful exercise. It was really pen-printing.

We were compelled to write very slowly and with the greatest precision. Any carelessness was sure to be followed by the ferule or rod. We were taught the bold, round hand. It was considered superior for copying and for records.

2. *Spelling.*—Spelling in that day was the foundation of all learning. A boy or girl was no scholar until he or she could spell well. Great interest was taken in "getting the spelling lesson." But few branches were taught, and spelling could have its full share of time and study. The *ologies* had not then made claim to a place in the public school course. Generally, classes stood around the room and spelled for head. Sometimes the school would take half an afternoon, and divide, one side spelling the other down. Often one school would send a challenge to another, and when thus met it was a time of deepest interest. These were never-to-be-forgotten times. No wonder the "old folks," last year, revived the spelling schools. They awakened precious memories.

3. *Reading.*—In the early day in Indiana no child was expected to try to read until he could spell well. We went through the spelling book two or three times before we commenced the lesson "No man may put off the Law of God," in Webster's spelling-book. We could then read without stammering. Webb's Word Method had not been invented. It mattered not how meaningless were the words, or how little thought was induced by the lesson, spelling must be studied for months and often years before reading was begun.

The perfect ideal of that day was loud and fast reading—the *faster* the *better.* We had some splendid readers! One young man, in particular, who had a clear, musical voice, and a rapid enunciation, often read John Gilpin. His reading was in perfect accord with the race. He was just the boy for the poem; and when he read, the school was entranced. How much we wished it had been longer, or that he would read it again!

We often had half as many classes as readers. We took for reading books whatever we had at home. For many years Murray's Readers were the only school series. The New Testament was more generally used than any other class-book. People in that day were not afraid of the Bible in school. Its exclusion is a modern policy. I remember well, on one occasion, we had a very large Testament class, and that each might be able to read more the class was divided, and both divisions recited at the same time in different parts of the room. We commenced a race to the end of Revelations. Never, perhaps, was the New Testament read so vigorously. Much as that holy book was thus thoughtlessly abused, impressions were made on the mind for good that were never forgotten. It is a book that whether well or illy used, will sow good seed in the heart of the reader. While he may expose his weakness, the Book is accomplishing its mission uninjured. Such reading was like the preaching at Philippi. Paul rejoiced that the gospel was *preached*, "whether in pretense or in truth." The Bible will have a good influence wherever it goes, however used or abused. It was thus honored and valued by the fathers of our State.

4. *Arithmetic.*—Arithmetic was regarded as the most important, because the most *practical* science. Every

business man desired to be "quick at figures," hence its value was high in the estimation of all. Commercial schools did not exist, and scientific book-keeping was not then taught. The "cyphering book" was the great preparation for business. Arithmetic was mainly taught from it, each pupil making a copy from the "*Masters*." The cyphering book was the best evidence of scholastic success, and whoever could turn out the best one was himself best.

It was common for teachers in the early day to have their scholars skip fractions, "since they were rarely used in business." Such teachers only took their classes to the "Rule of Three." When they got to "Practice," fractions had to be studied. There were probably good and untold reasons for "skipping" this subject.

The idea generally prevailed that girls had little need for arithmetic beyond "Reduction," and their course was very brief. When a young man became an expert in arithmetic, he was much prized as a teacher. He was the neighborhood prodigy.

5. *Grammar.*—Murray's Grammar was the standard work for this science up to 1830. His course consisted of a small book containing the rudiments, a larger work, and Exercises in False Syntax. We had to commit to memory the coarse print and the rules, and stand in the middle of the room to "say it." If we failed, a dose of beech stimulant was administered, and the lesson given again. Another failure was met by another dose, and so we went on and on. The reader may think he could not learn by that method. He is mistaken. I have tried it, and I ought to know. Whether it is the best method or not is another ques-

tion. I am willing that other methods should take its place.

Murray, in time, was supplanted by Kirkham. His work was written in an easy and familiar style, and rapidly popularized the science. In a few years, publishers began to make books according to the "best methods," and a fierce and persistent book war was begun. Each had the best and the latest. It was soon found that there was more in the man who pressed the book upon the market, than in the book itself; and publishers were wise and shrewd enough to select the best men for their agents. Our schools became oppressed with a heterogeneous supply; each family claiming the right to use such books as it had, though brought from North Carolina, Virginia, or New England, teachers were unable to reduce their work to any system. Their labor was largely wasted. By the general revision of the school laws in 1852, school officers were authorized to secure uniformity of textbooks, and teachers were enabled to classify their schools and thus to economize their instruction.

6. *Geography.*—I can remember well when Morse's Geography came into the State. It was about the year 1825. It created a great sensation. It was a period in school history. Before this, but few had a clear idea of the earth's rotundity. Many could not understand the subject well enough to reason upon it. Many were emphatic and persistent in repudiating the absurd idea that the world is round, and turns over. Debating clubs discussed the subject, and to the opposition it was perfectly clear that if the world turned over we would *all fall off*, and the water in the ocean would be spilled out. Morse's Geography cleared

away the fog; and when Comstock's Philosophy, with its brief outline of astronomy, was introduced, the school-boy could understand the subject well. Morse's work being too large and expensive, it was soon supplanted by Woodbridge's, which had a deservedly good sale. It was a superior work for the times. Soon the book war came on, and each school had a beautiful variety.

Uniformity of Class Books.—In 1857, an effort was made to secure a uniformity of class books for the State, by the State Board of Education. Selections were made and recommended for use in the schools of the State. This move carried the subject to the other extreme, and required a change too radical to be successful.

Exercise and Amusements.—"Free Gymnastics" was preferred by the pioneer schools. They chose the open air for their sports. "Bull pen" was a favorite game. They liked to hit each other with the ball, so that it could be felt. Good dodging required the play of every muscle. Town-ball, base, and cat were favorite games. Foot-ball was rarely played in the early school days. Marbles was a hot-weather game. Wrestling and jumping were the games to test activity and strength, and were favorites with those who expected to come off best. These sports were healthful and very enjoyable. The sturdy pioneers, whose work was largely felling trees and clearing land, greatly enjoyed tests of activity and strength.

Mixed Schools.—It will be observed that in 1824, the school law required that the schools of the State "shall be forever open for the education of all children within the district without distinction." Virginia had ceded the North-west Territory to the United States on condition that its citizens should forever enjoy the same freedom as those of other States; and when Indiana was organized as a Territory, and afterwards as a State, this obligation was expressly recognized as binding; hence, the full and impartial language of the statute.

Colored children were found in many public schools in common with white children. Comparatively little prejudice was manifested towards them until about the year 1830, when abolition sentiments created a sensation in the nation. They were then generally excluded from the free schools of the State. Their rights have been again restored by the Fifteenth Amendment to the Constitution of the United States, and in 1869 special legislation was made in their favor.

My First School.—In the autumn of 1833, a year made memorable by the "meteoric shower" in the United States, when I had just reached eighteen years, in Bartholomew county, eight miles south of Columbus, where the most valuable sixteenth section in the State is found, the rents of which support the schools ten months in the year, I taught my first school. I could not have found a better place in which to begin. The whole neighborhood was made of good material, socially, financially, and religiously. My school numbered about forty, and twenty-five of them were from five families. Many of these, both girls and boys, were older than myself. One young lady of twenty or more, recited in the spelling-book. The recollection of this school calls up many pleasing memories and lasting friendships.

County Seminaries.—The pioneer legislators of

Indiana conceived an educational system that should meet the entire wants of the people. The common school was to be its base, and the State University its apex. The County Seminary was to fill the space between and furnish a preparatory course for the University. The conception was good in theory, but did not succeed well in practice. The failure was caused by a general want of successful educators at the head of the county seminaries who could draw support and build them up. Successful men rarely continued in the business. They found greater profit and honor in medicine and law, or in trade. In Salem, Washington County, there was an exception to this rule. Under the instruction and good management of the Hon. John I. Morrison, since Treasurer of State, and now President of the University Board of Trustees, an academy was successfully sustained for nearly two decades of years. It exerted a wide influence in the State, and its good work has since borne fruit in many other States. Its students were of both sexes, and its success, in this respect, has put to rest, in the minds of those who were there educated, doubts of the economy or desirability of co-education. Hundreds in Indiana can recur with pleasure to the wholesome influences and incentives received at this institution, myself among the number.

WHAT OF ALL THIS?—Much every way. When I look back through the half century of experiences, trials, failures and successes, memory becomes crowded with incidents that tell of mutation, progress, development. We see a sovereign State rising from infancy to manhood. Our fathers looked forward to a grand culmination of all the appliances embraced in their wise system. The "log cabin" has passed away, and the neat frame or brick building has taken its place. The old, rickety and rough bench, without a back, has given place to the elegant desk and settee. Instead of the untidy school-room, with its puncheon floor and miserable furnishings, we now have the tasteful edifice, supplied with all the educational appliances that utility and educational economy can furnish. Old things have passed away, and all things have become new. The State is rising in strength and power, and will make no backward move. Her rich soil, the incalculable wealth of her mines, her net-work of railways, her heavy forests, her central commercial position in the industries and exchange of the nation, her industry and prosperity, all tell what her future must be. May her sons and daughters be worthy of their sires. If so much has been done in sixty years, what may we expect at her hundredth anniversary,—in 1916?

The time has passed when the teacher should be considered a fit subject for the ridicule of the essayist. States and nations must see that where the work of the common school is well done, there are pleasant homes, industry, happiness, and wealth. Contentment comes to the laborer when he sees that worthy, intelligent, God-fearing men and women are molding the minds of his children for useful and happy lives.

Men and nations are as they are taught. As a people elevate and sustain their educators, so will their educators be found, in turn, the great instrumentality which brings them intelligence, freedom, prosperity, and peace, and in the end true honor and glory.

SCHOOL LEGISLATION.

BY

JOHN M. OLCOTT, A. M.

SCHOOL LEGISLATION.

WHEN the successful termination of the Revolutionary War gave to a free people the control of a great nation, the fact that the safety and welfare of the nation depended on the general intelligence and virtue of the people, was so evident that nearly all of the several states of the Union began to provide means for the encouragement and support of popular education; and the general government adopted the policy of making munificent donations of public lands for the support of common schools. In this policy of the general government we find the corner-stone of the Indiana State system of free public schools.

On the 20th of May, 1785, Congress passed an ordinance in relation to the mode of disposing of the public lands in the territory of the United States, northwest of the Ohio River. This territory embraced within its boundaries all the lands which are now included within the limits of Ohio, Indiana, Illinois, Michigan, and Wisconsin, together with that part of Minnesota which lies on the left bank of the Mississippi river.

The ordinance of May 20th, 1785, declared that one square mile of land, or section No. 16, in every township should be reserved for the maintenance of public schools. The third article of compact in the Ordinance of Congress, of July 13, 1787, declares that "religion, morality, and knowledge, being necessary to the good government and the happiness of mankind, schools and the means of education shall forever be encouraged."

By these national acts a great principle was asserted and established, and the thirty-sixth part of all lands, within the immense North-western Territory, was devoted to the maintenance of common schools for the education of the people.

TERRITORIAL LEGISLATION.—In the course of the territorial existence of Indiana, the subject of schools, for the instruction of youth, was often pressed upon the attention of the people by the friends of popular education. But, from the time of the organization of the territorial government until the adoption of a State constitution, in 1816, the constant presence of insurmountable difficulties prevented the establishment of any system of common school education.

In 1807, the General Assembly of the territory passed an act to incorporate "the Vincennes University, for the instruction of youth in the Latin, Greek, French, and English languages, mathematics, natural philosophy, ancient and modern history, moral philosophy, logic, rhetoric, and the law of nature and nations." In the preamble to this act, the territorial legislature declared that the independence, happiness, and energy of every republic depended (under the influences of the destinies of heaven) upon the wisdom, virtue, talents, and energy of its citizens and rulers; and that science, literature, and the liberal arts contributed, in an eminent degree, to improve those qualities and acquirements; and that learning had ever been found the ablest advocate of genuine liberty, the best supporter of rational religion, and the source of the only solid and imperishable glory which nations can acquire.

By an act of the General Assembly of October 26, 1808, the several courts of common pleas within the Indiana Territory were invested with full power to lease the sections of land which had been reserved in the respective counties for the use of schools, upon the terms best calculated to promote the improvement of the land. An act of the Legislature, of December 14, 1810, authorized the courts of common pleas to appoint, in the several counties, trustees of the school lands. This act prohibited the leasing to any person of more than one quarter section, or one hundred and sixty acres. The destruction of sugar trees, and the waste of other timber growing on the school lands were prohibited.

There was no further important legislation on the subject of common schools during the existence of the territorial government.

First State Constitution.—That part of the ninth article of the Constitution of 1816 pertaining to common schools is in these words:

"Knowledge and learning generally diffused through a community, being essential to the preservation of a free government, and spreading the opportunities and advantages of education through the various parts of the country being highly conducive to this end, it shall be the duty of the General Assembly to provide by law for the improvement of such lands as are, or hereafter may be, granted by the United States to this state for the use of schools, and to apply any funds which may be raised from such lands, or from any other quarter, to the accomplishment of the grand object for which they are or may be intended; but no lands granted for the use of schools or seminaries of learning shall be sold by authority of this State prior to the year eighteen hundred and twenty; and the moneys which may be raised out of the sale of any such lands, or otherwise obtained for the purposes aforesaid, shall be and remain a fund for the exclusive purpose of promoting the interest of literature and the sciences, and for the support of seminaries and public schools.

"It shall be the duty of the General Assembly, as soon as circumstances will permit, to provide by law for a general system of education, ascending in a regular gradation from township schools to a State university, wherein tuition shall be gratis and equally open to all. And for the promotion of such salutary end, the money which shall be paid as an equivalent by persons exempt from military duty, except in times of war, shall be exclusively, and in equal proportion, applied to the support of county seminaries; also all fines assessed for any breach of the penal laws shall be applied to said seminaries in the counties wherein they shall be assessed."

For a long period after the adoption of the first State Constitution, the founding of any effective public school system in Indiana was rendered impracticable by the presence of obstacles which the friends of popular education could neither overcome nor remove.

Among these obstacles were the want of funds to build school-houses and to pay teachers, the sparseness of the population in school districts, the mismanagement of school funds, the opposition of the few and the indifference of the many, and the general condition of the pioneer settlers, which was such as to require for the greater part of each year the assistance of the younger members of the family in the work of clearing away the forests, opening the farms, and planting, cultivating, and gathering crops. Still, amid all these difficulties, the friends of a general system of public instruction continued to work and to look forward with hopes of ultimate success.

By an act of the General Assembly of December 14, 1816, provision was made for the appointment of superintendents of school sections in the several townships. These superintendents were authorized to lease school lands for any term not exceeding seven years. Every lessee of such lands was required to set out each year twenty-five apple and twenty-five peach trees, until one hundred of each had been planted. Between the years 1816 and 1820 several laws were passed for the incorporation of academies, seminaries, and literary associations.

By a joint resolution of the General Assembly of Jan. 9, 1821, John Badollet and David Hart, of Knox County; William W. Martin, of Washington County; James Welsh, of Switzerland County; Daniel S. Caswell, of Franklin County; Thomas C. Searle, of Jefferson County; and John Todd, of Clarke County, were appointed a committee to draft and report to the next Legislature of Indiana a bill providing for a general system of education; and they were instructed to guard particularly against "any distinction between the *rich* and *poor*." The labors of the committee thus appointed, after having passed under the revision of Judge Benjamin Parke and the General Assembly, were incorporated in the first general school law of Indiana, which appears in the revised statutes of 1824 under the title of "an act to incorporate congressional townships and providing for public schools therein."

This law required the inhabitants of each congressional township to meet at the section reserved by Congress for the use of schools, or at some place convenient thereto, to elect three persons of their township as trustees who were vested with the general control of school lands, with power to divide their respective congressional townships into geographical school districts, appoint sub-trustees for the same, and to manage the school lands and schools generally. This law provided for building school-houses, in these words: "Every able-bodied male person of the age of twenty-one years and upwards residing within the bounds of such school district, shall be liable to work one day in each week until such building may be completed, or pay the sum of thirty-seven and one-half cents for every day he may so fail to work." The same act describes a school-house in these words: "In all cases such school-house shall be eight feet between the floors, and at least one foot from the surface of the ground to the first floor, and finished in a manner calculated to render comfortable the teacher and pupils, etc."

The trustees examined teachers with respect to their ability to teach reading, writing, and arithmetic. Occasionally schools were established, continuing two or three months, and sustained by rate bills. They were *not free.*

At almost every session of the Legislature, until the adoption of the new constitution in 1851, either special or general laws have been passed on the subject of common schools, or in reference to the incorporation of seminaries, academies, colleges, universities, or libraries. A great many important and complex questions having reference to school laws, school funds, school lands, etc., had been raised and brought before the courts to be decided. Yet there were no free schools.

A vast amount of labor had been performed by private citizens, by legislatures and committees, by state conventions and county meetings, by meetings in townships and in school districts, to establish and maintain a permanent system of State schools entirely free and equally open to all; still, for a period of thirty-six years after the adoption of the first State constitution, school officers could do little more than to *encourage* schools. They possessed neither means nor authority to build school-houses or to establish schools. They could not levy a tax to build school-houses except by special permission of the district, and even then the amount of the money appropriation was limited by the Legislature of 1834 to fifty dollars for each school-house. Teachers were poorly qualified, and there were no means at hand for their improvement.

But the pioneer settlements of this great State were not without far-seeing and noble-hearted individuals who were constrained to labor for the far distant future, and who were willing to wait for results. They planned wiser than they knew in providing for an accumulative common school fund which is now larger than that possessed by any other State by *more than two millions of dollars.*

ORIGIN OF THE SCHOOL FUND.—This immense school

fund, now approximating nine million dollars, which is the solid rock in the center of the foundation of our present school system, has accumulated from the following sources:

1. The Congressional Township Fund;
2. The Bank Tax Fund;
3. The Sinking Fund;
4. The Surplus Revenue Fund;
5. The Saline Fund;
6. The Swamp Land Fund;
7. The Seminary Fund;
8. The Contingent Fund.

The source of the Congressional Township Fund has already been mentioned.

By the fifteenth section of the charter of the State Bank of Indiana, in the year 1834, it was provided that "There shall be deducted from the dividends and retained in Bank each year the sum of twelve and one-half cents on each share of stocks, other than that held by the State, which shall constitute part of the permanent fund to be devoted to purposes of common school education under the direction of the General Assembly, and shall be suffered to remain in bank and accumulate until such appropriation by the General Assembly." This is known as the Bank Tax Fund, and it has yielded to the school fund $80,000, which is now bearing interest in favor of education.

The same act of 1834, establishing the State Bank of Indiana, provided that the State should borrow for twenty years or more, at a rate of interest not exceeding five per cent, $1,300,000. Of this sum, $800,000 was appropriated to the payment of the stock in the bank, being one-half of the whole capital of the bank.

The remaining $500,000 was designed to be loaned to individuals at six per cent per annum for a long term of years, to assist them in paying for their portion of the stock in bank.

The same act provided that the semi-annual payments of interest on this loan to individuals, the funds which should eventually be received in payment of their loans, and the dividends declared and paid by the bank on the State stocks, together with any part of the State loan not required for paying the State stock in bank, should constitute a sinking fund, reserved and set apart, principal and interest, for the purpose of paying off the loan negotiated on the part of the State, and the interest thereon. The residue of the fund after the payment of the loan, interest and expenses, was ordered to form a permanent fund appropriated to the cause of common school education. This provision has yielded to the common school fund about five and a half millions of dollars, which constitute the present Sinking Fund.

Under the administration of President Jackson the national debt, contracted by the Revolutionary War and the purchase of Louisiana, was entirely discharged, and a surplus remained in the treasury. Congress in June, 1836, distributed this money among the states in the ratio of their representation in Congress. The sum of eight hundred and sixty thousand two hundred and fifty-four dollars was Indiana's share. The Legislature, by an act approved February 6, 1837, set apart five hundred and seventy-three thousand five hundred and two dollars and ninety-six cents as a permanent part of the school fund, and designated it, Surplus Revenue Fund.

Section second of article eighth of our State Constitution provides that: "All lands which have been or may hereafter be granted to the State, when no special purpose is expressed in the grant, and the proceeds of the sales thereof, including the proceeds of the sales of the swamp lands granted to the State of Indiana by the act of Congress of the 28th of September, 1850, after deducting the expenses of selecting and draining the same," shall be a part of the common school fund. Congress having granted to the State large tracts of swamp lands, and having expressed no purpose in the grant, the State was at liberty to dispose of them for any purpose she might see proper. She ordered that these lands be sold, expenses paid out of the proceeds, and the remainder converted into a common school fund called the Swamp Land Fund.

By an act of Congress, passed in 1816, it was provided that all salt springs within the Indiana territory, and the land reserved for the use of the same, not exceeding in the whole thirty-six entire sections, should be granted to the State for the use of the people, under such conditions, terms, and regulations as the Legislature should direct. In 1832, Congress authorized the Legislature to sell these lands and appropriate the proceeds to the support of the common schools. This produced the Saline Fund, and yielded to the Common School Fund $85,000.

In 1852, the Legislature ordered the sale of all county seminaries and property, real and personal, belonging thereto, and provided that the net proceeds of the sales should be placed to the credit of the Common School Fund. It is impossible to state just how much has been realized from this source.

Under the head of Contingent Funds may be classed all funds arising from the provisions of the Legislature concerning fines, forfeitures, escheats, etc. The yield from this source can not be definitely stated.

The several sources above enumerated have yielded, up to this date, about nine millions of dollars, which "may be increased, but shall never be diminished; and the income thereof shall be inviolably appropriated to the support of common schools and to no other purpose whatever."

LATER LEGISLATION.—It is true that in 1837 the General Assembly had provided for the election of a County School Commissioner, and in 1843 it had provided that the State Treasurer should perform the duties of Superintendent of Public Instruction; but neither of these officers were permitted, under the law, to do any thing looking to the establishment of a general system of schools.

It was not until after the adoption of the new constitution, in 1851, that any positive legislation was obtained for the establishment of common schools, entirely free, and under the exclusive management of the State.

Previous to that time the school officers were dependent upon the uncertain popular vote of a district, township, town, or city for instructions concerning the sale or lease of school lands, the loaning of money, the building of school-houses, and the employment of teachers—all of which had a tendency to render the founding of free schools precarious and unpromising. The people depended upon private schools, academies, and seminaries.

The new constitutional provision for the establishment of "a general and uniform system of common schools, wherein tuition shall be without charge and equally open to all," was accepted by a majority vote of more than eighty thousand. The statutory form and expression given to the new constitution, entitled "an act to provide for a general and uniform system of common schools and school libraries," approved June 14, 1852, was the first law which made it possible to build up a system of State schools worthy the name, and the first step toward putting into execution the constitutional provision proclaimed thirty-six years before.

The school law of 1852 was exceedingly liberal in many respects, and embodied in its provisions fundamental principles and practical excellencies unsurpassed by the legislative wisdom of any sister State. This law embodied the principles that the property of the State should educate the children of the State, and that all common schools should be open to the pupils thereof without charge. The first section of this act provided for levying and collecting a property tax of ten cents on each one hundred dollars. The second section provided for the consolidation and general management by the State of all school funds heretofore mentioned.

This law abolished the congressional township system, and declared each civil township a township for school purposes, and the trustees thereof trustees for school purposes, and gave them full charge of the educational affairs of the township. They were empowered to build school-houses, establish graded-schools, employ teachers, etc., as circumstances seemed to require. The law provided for a better investment of the common school fund, and made the several counties responsible for the preservation of the same, and for the payment of the annual interest thereon. It provided for the election of a State Superintendent of Public Instruction, fixing the term of office at two years, and his salary at $500 per annum. It provided for the organization of a State Board of Education in the following words:

"The State Board of Education shall consist of the State Superintendent of Public Instruction, the Governor, the Secretary, Treasurer, and Auditor of State, who shall meet annually, at Indianapolis, on the second Monday of November, for the purpose of more effectually promoting the interests of education, by mutual conference, interchange of views, and experience of the practical operation of the system, the introduction of uniform school books, the adoption of the most eligible means of facilitating the establishment of township school libraries, and the discussion and determination of such questions as may arise in the practical administration of the school system."

It provided for the purchase of township school libraries, under the direction of the State Board of Education, levying for that purpose a property tax of "one quarter of one mill on each one dollar," and a poll tax of twenty-five cents.

Section 32 declared incorporated cities and towns to be school corporations, independent of the townships in which they may be situated, entitled to the proportional amount of school funds, and authorized to appoint independent trustees, with power to establish graded-schools and power to levy taxes for their support, after the public funds shall have been exhausted, and to build school-houses, etc.

Section 130 reads as follows: "The voters of any township shall have power at any general or special meeting to vote a tax for the purpose of building or repairing school-houses, and purchasing sites therefor, providing fuel, furniture, maps, apparatus, libraries or increase thereof, or to discharge debts incurred therefor, and for continuing their schools, after the public funds shall have been expended, to any amount not exceeding annually fifty cents on each one hundred dollars of property, and fifty cents on each poll."

These two sections, exceedingly broad and liberal in spirit, as were the views of the legislators who made them, at once charged the whole educational machinery of the state with a new life. School-houses, large and commodious, were erected in the larger cities. Graded-schools were established in rapid succession. Everywhere hope, enterprise, activity, the true spirit of educational progress and enthusiasm, prevailed; but in a very few years the State's rapid progress in building up a system of free common schools was checked by contentions concerning the constitutionality of these very sections. In the cause of Greencastle Township in Putnam County and Kercheval, County Treasurer, *versus* Black, the court held that section 130, quoted above, was repugnant to the constitution, in that it provided for taxation which was not "*general and uniform.*" Section 32, which gave similar power to incorporated towns and cities, was, for like reason, overruled by the court in the case of the city of Lafayette *versus* William M. Jenners.

The effect of these decisions was to render inoperative all efforts to sustain graded-schools, of which many had just gone into successful operation in the larger towns and cities, and which were beginning to realize the best hopes of their founders. These schools were too young to withstand the withering blight of legal obstacles, calling in question the constitutionality of the very basis of their prosperity. They were discontinued for a time, but the recuperative power and energy of determined teachers and friends of education were such that, by the celerity of their movements, before a retreat was ordered, they inaugurated a movement to remove the disturbing elements of a constitutional character and to restore public confidence, hoping thus to save the schools from utter destruction.

A State Teachers' Association was organized, for the determined purpose of discussing the great fundamental principles of an educational system and the appropriate instrumentalities to be employed. The results of the discussions and deliberations of this body, in the varied forms of memorials, petitions, resolutions, and advisory committees, have not only found their way to the legislative halls, but have there so influenced and guided subsequent legislation, that, for practical wisdom, the present Indiana School System has no superior among the states. At the second meeting of the association an educational periodical was established, called the "*Indiana School Journal*," which has always advocated the fittest legislation for common schools, and persistently pressed law-makers to a sense of duty whenever active measures were required.

These efforts of the friends of education resulted in the passage of the new school law of 1865, which breathed life and hope into our whole educational system. While the decision of the Supreme Court, above referred to, has never been overruled, the law of 1865 remains unchallenged by this highest judicial tribunal. One of the sections of the act of 1865 provided for the establishment of Teachers' Institutes, and required the appropriation of the sum of $50 annually in each county for support of the same. This provision gave a new impulse to the cause of education, which permeated the entire system of State schools, infusing activity and energy and ennobling aspirations through all its course. The County Teachers' Institute in Indiana has proved to be the engine of power by which the teachers, the common schools, and the State as a whole, have been elevated from gross darkness to the clear sunlight of midday. No other one instrumentality has done so much to raise the standard of teaching, to popularize the public schools, to establish among the masses a healthy educational sentiment, and to create a thirst for knowledge, as the County Teachers' Institute.

It has already been stated that the teachers of the State have inaugurated the most important measures pertaining to substantial progress in school legislation. In 1855, their association appointed a committee to memorialize the legislature with reference to the establishment of Normal Schools. This was followed by repeated discussions, resolutions, and the appointment of conference committees at almost every annual session of the association for ten consecutive years, without apparent fruit.

The several and successive State Superintendents of Public Instruction, for an equal number of years, presented in their annual reports elaborate and exhaustive arguments and statistics, urging upon the General Assembly the necessity of making some provision for the better education of teachers. By the gratuitous labors and the most persistent efforts of individual teachers, a State Normal Institute was organized in 1865, which continued in operation for a period of four weeks. Other State Institutes were afterwards held, which did much to stimulate the public sentiment now being formed in favor of Normal Schools.

On the 20th day of December, 1865, the General Assembly finally consented to put in statutory form the progressive sentiment thus created, and established a State Normal School, locating it in the city of Terre Haute. One hundred and seventy-nine thousand dollars have been expended on the buildings alone, and the school is now in successful operation. The State University at Bloomington, organized in 1834, stands at the head of our public school system. It is liberally endowed by the State, sustaining a law school and a medical school. The agricultural school is located at Lafayette, and is called the Purdue University. This school is in its infancy.

Of the more recent legislation, which has proved beneficial to the school system, may be mentioned the increase of the property tax in 1865 from ten to sixteen cents on the hundred dollars, the local and special tax provisions of 1865 and 1867, the provision for educating the colored children of the State, and the law of 1869, empowering trustees to issue bonds for building purposes.

The education of the colored children was provided for May 13, 1869, as follows: Sec. 3. "The trustee or trustees of each township, town, or city, shall organize the colored children into separate schools, having all the rights and privileges of other schools of the township; *Provided,* There are not a sufficient number within attending distance, the several districts may be consolidated and form one district. But if there are not a sufficient number within reasonable distance to be thus consolidated, the trustee or trustees shall provide such other means of education for said children as shall use their proportion, according to number, of school revenue to the best advantage."

By an act of the Legislature, approved March 8, 1873, the office of County Superintendent was created, and the general management of all the schools in each county was placed under the control of this officer. The same law provided for a County Board of Education to consist of the county superintendent, the trustees of the townships, and the school trustees of the towns and cities of the county. It also made provision for Township Institutes in these words, viz.: "At least one Saturday in each month, during which the public schools may be in progress, shall be devoted to Township Institutes or model schools for the improvement of Teachers, and two Saturdays may be appropriated at the discretion of the Township Trustee of any township; . . . . . . The Township Trustee shall specify in a written contract with each teacher, that such teacher shall attend the full session of each Institute contemplated therein, or forfeit one day's wages for every day's absence therefrom, unless such absence shall be occasioned by sickness." This provision is accomplishing much good for the schools.

The State Board of Education now consists of the following officers, viz.:—

1. The State Superintendent of Public Instruction.
2. The Governor of the State.

3. The President of the State University.
4. The President of Purdue University.
5. The President of the State Normal School.
6. The Superintendent of Public Schools in the three largest cities in the State.

This Board has power to grant State license to teachers found eminently qualified upon examination; to prepare uniform questions to be used by county superintendents in their examination of teachers; to appoint trustees of the State University and the examiners of the State Normal School; and to exercise a general management of the public school interests of the State.

The Indiana public school system at this time may be epitomized by the presentation of its officers in regular order as follows, viz.:

1. State Superintendent of Public Instruction, elected by the people.
2. State Board of Education, *ex officio*.
3. County Superintendents, appointed by the County Commissioner.
4. Township Trustees, elected by the people.
5. City and Town Trustees, appointed by the City Council or Town Trustees.
6. School Commissioner for cities above thirty thousand inhabitants, elected by the people.

OUR EMINENT EDUCATORS.

BY

DANIEL HOUGH.

OUR EMINENT EDUCATORS.

AS only a limited number of pages could be allowed for these sketches, the writer has left out all that did not directly illustrate the subject. If any feel a regret that their particular friends or teachers have not here a place, the writer can say that an appeal was made to every county for data, but that in many instances there was no response. Among these sketches will be found the olden time school-masters, teachers of private schools, of county seminaries, college presidents and professors, city superintendents, and state superintendents.

The writer was born in this State nearly half a century ago, and was therefore brought up under the instruction of the old school-masters, and he can truly bear testimony to their humanity. He never went to a brutal teacher. Feeling thus, this work of attempting to perpetuate their memory has been one of love.

TEACHERS OF THE EARLIER DAYS.—The first school-teacher in Indiana, of which we have any account, was M. RIVET, a polite, liberal-minded missionary, who was driven out of Europe by the French Revolution. He came to America and opened a school at Vincennes, about the year 1793.

The next school, of which we learn, was taught in Clarke County, near Charlestown, in 1803. The text-books were "Dilworth's Spelling Book," "Gulliver's Travels," and a "Dream Book." Rev. Geo. K. Hester was a pupil in this school in 1804. The school was "kept from sun to sun," with a "play-time" at noon, and the pupil that came first "said his lesson first."

JULIA L. DUMONT, daughter of Ebenezer and Martha D. Corey, was born October, 1794, at Waterford, Washington County, Ohio. Her father dying during her infancy, her mother removed to Greenfield, Saratoga County, N. Y. She studied at Milton Academy, in that county, where her superior mental powers gave promise of her future success in life. In 1811 she taught her first school in Greenfield, and in 1812 her second in Cambridge, Washington County, N. Y. In August of this year she was married to John Dumont, and soon after removed to Vevay, Indiana, where she continued to reside until her death, January 2, 1857. At Vevay she had a room built for the purpose in her dwelling, in which she opened a school which was a model for all the region round about. Few teachers equaled her in energy and thoroughness, or in the power of awakening and keeping up in the minds of their pupils a lively and continued interest in their studies. Many of the childish essays of her former pupils, still carefully preserved by them, show in the corrections by her own hand how indefatigable she was. They show, too, that those whom she taught had to digest and know thoroughly every lesson. Her loving heart and tireless efforts brought success where others failed. Her care for the weak in body or mind was only such as a mother could give. The writer has often met her former pupils, and it was ever a joy to him to hear them tell of her great heart and of her many excellencies. With all the duties of teacher, she bore those of wife, mother, nurse, and housekeeper, and besides was a voluminous writer for the press, both in prose and poetry.

WILLIAM HAUGHTON, a teacher of over fifty years standing in Indiana, and a minister of the Society of Friends, was born in 1803, in Ireland, and was educated at a Friends' boarding-school, in Ackworth England. At the age of eighteen he emigrated to America. He first taught in Fayette County, Indiana, where two of his sisters resided. He then removed to Union County, where he continued his work as teacher. Wishing to secure the benefit of his instruction to their own families, two worthy farmers, Stephen Butler and Thomas Hollingsworth, erected *Beech Grove Seminary*, two miles south from Liberty, and employed Friend Haughton as principal. He now married, and continued as principal of the seminary until 1848, or for twenty-one years. This was a worthy English school in all respects, and was attended by earnest young men and women, whose business it was to prepare for a life-work. Among the many educated there, the writer well remembers the following: General A. E. Burnside; Mrs. Hannah Hadley, the philanthropist of Indianapolis; Judge Hervey Cravens, Col. Nelson Trusler, Hon. R. M. Haworth, Judge Jonathan Gardner, Hon. E. Donelan, of Missouri; Dr. O. W. Nixon, of the Cincinnati *Times*, besides hosts of others not less known. Since 1848 he has taught in the Friends school at Whitewater (Richmond), in the Friends boarding-school near Richmond, now Earlham College, at Knightstown, and at Raysville, where he now resides. He now teaches in the Knightstown Graded Schools, and apparently with as much vigor as forty years ago. Both as teacher and minister he is loved by all who respect a good man.

TANDY BAILEY MONTGOMERY was one of the old schoolmasters of southwestern Indiana. He was born in Kentucky in 1809, and died in Princeton, Indiana, 1862. In his boyhood he was lamed for life, and on this account his brothers assisted him in getting an English education, so that he might live by teaching. He attended school at New Harmony in "Community times," hence he received the rare favor of instruction in the Pestalozzian system. He commenced teaching at the age of fourteen, and his entire experience amounted to twenty years. His early work was in subscription schools in Gibson, Warrick, and Pike Counties. The price paid Mr. Montgomery for his services was $1.50 per quarter for each scholar. His reputation as a thorough scholar and successful teacher soon enabled him to get $2.00 to $2.50 per quarter. When teaching for public money, he always commanded the highest price, receiving on one occasion *ninety dollars for one quarter!* In 1860, he was elected Recorder of Gibson County, in which capacity he was serving when he died.

REV. BAYARD R. HALL, A.M., was the first teacher in the State Seminary, which afterwards grew into the Indiana State University, at Bloomington. He commenced his work there in 1824, at a salary of $150 per year. In 1828, the school was organized into the

"Indiana College," and Mr. Hall was made Professor of Latin and Greek, which position he held till 1832, when he returned East and became principal of the Classical and Mathematical Institute at Newburgh, N. Y. He subsequently settled in Brooklyn, where he died a few years ago. He was the author of several books, among which may be mentioned "Teaching a Science, the Teacher an Artist," "The New Purchase," and "Something for Everybody."

The following were early teachers in Fort Wayne: Mr. McCoy, assisted by Mr. Montgomery and Mr. and Mrs. Potts, taught in the old fort as early as 1821.

In 1825 the County Seminary was built, and in it the following teachers taught, viz.: Jno. P. Hedges, in 1826; Henry Cooper and Mr. Boggs; and the record says they were followed by "*others.*" From 1832 to 1836 we have Mr. Auchinbaugh, Smallwood Noel, James Requa, Myron F. Barbour, and John C. Sivey. In 1836 Miss Mann, now Mrs. Ex-Sec'y McCulloch, and Miss Hubbell, afterwards Mrs. R. W. Taylor, were the teachers. These were followed by Jesse Hoover, Rev. W. W. Stevens, Alexander McJunkin, Mrs. Lydia Sykes, Rev. James Greer, and Prof. A. C. Heustis, who concluded the pioneer work.

The following were pioneer teachers in Lafayette: Joseph Talman, 1827; John D. Farmer, 1828; Hugh McKing, 1829; Ezekiel Simmons, 1830; Abigail Huff, 1833; and Rev. Joseph Wilson, the first seminary teacher, in 1841.

JOHN I. MORRISON was born in 1806, in Franklin County, Pa. He moved to Indiana in 1826, and settled at Salem, Washington County. Here he established a school, which became widely known for the sound practical learning and accurate scholarship of its pupils, of whom we have space to mention but very few of the many who are well known throughout the State, viz.: Elijah Newland, John Gordon, Edward Albertson, Thomas J. Rodman, Robt. Allen, William Dewey, Minard Sturgus, Zebulon B. Sturgus, Jno. L. Campbell, Barnabas C. Hobbs, Jas. G. May, Washington DePauw, Sam'l Reid, Nathan Kimball, J. J. Talbott, Newton Booth, etc. In 1835 he built and established the Salem Female Institute. He was a professor in the State University three years. He served in both branches of the State Legislature, and was a member of the Constitutional Convention. As chairman of the Committee on Education, he reported substantially the article on Education, and was sole author of the section creating the office of State Superintendent of Public Instruction. He was twice elected Treasurer of Washington County; was appointed by President Lincoln Commissioner of Enrollment, and while in that office was elected Treasurer of State. He is now President of the Board of Trustees of the State University, and Secretary of the school board at Knightstown, where he resides. In all these varied positions he has ever been known as a faithful officer, who has never swerved from the path of duty.

Ebenezer Sharpe came to Indianapolis in 1826, and the same year established a school. Mr. Sharpe at once took a position as a citizen of the first order of merit, and as a teacher of rare ability and worth. He is spoken of by his now gray-headed pupils as a man of culture and accomplishments. By his excellence in his profession he gave tone to popular education in the minds of the public. Many of the most estimable citizens of Indianapolis are indebted to his moral and religious counsels, as well as to his instruction in literature and science, for their success in after life.

Among the other ancient school-masters of Indianapolis deserving honorable mention are the following: Sam'l Merrill, Thomas D. Gregg, Rev. Wm. A. Holliday, James S. Kemper, Ebenezer Daumont, J. P. Safford, and Benj. Lang.

The first superintendent of Indianapolis schools was Silas T. Bowen, in 1855, formerly associate of D. P. Page, of the Albany (N. Y.) Normal School. His instructions were to visit each school once a month. Mr. Bowen is now a book-seller, of the firm of Bowen, Stewart & Co. The next year, 1856, Mr. Geo. B. Stone was appointed superintendent. All his time was given to the schools, and they were conducted with vigor and success until the disastrous decision of the Supreme Court, in 1858, to the effect that local taxation was unlawful. There being only sufficient funds for conducting the schools three months in the year, many of the leading teachers either went into other business or left the State. Among the latter was the energetic, conscientious Geo. B. Stone.

Rev. Hiram A. Hunter was one of the early Seminary teachers of Indiana, having taught most of the time from 1827 to 1834, at Washington, Logansport, and Princeton. He was born near Lynchburg, Va., August 13, 1800, and is still living in Louisville, Ky. He served as a member of General Jackson's body-guard in 1818 in the first Seminole War, and was a spectator to the execution of Arbuthnot and Ambrister, the capture of Forts St. Marks and Barancas, and the various events of that war that caused the difficulty with Spain and brought about the cession of Florida. He has been preaching more than fifty-six years, principally in Indiana and Kentucky, although he was several years pastor of a church in Philadelphia, Pa. He went to Logansport to deliver an address at the laying of the corner-stone of the Masonic Hall, in 1829, and he was, at that time, engaged to take charge of the Cass County Seminary, the first, and for some time the only, school in Cass County. Among his pupils were several Pottawattamie Indians.

SANFORD C. COX was born July 1, 1811, in Wayne County, Ind. He was a self-educated man. With his father he removed to Crawfordsville in 1824, and in the same year removed to Lafayette, where he commenced teaching in 1827. He next taught at Williamsport, then at Black, Montgomery County. While acting as "Black Creek school-master" his friends at home elected him Recorder for the county, which position he held twenty-two and a half years. He is the author of "Old Settlers on the Wabash," a work of historical reminiscences. He is an attorney, and still lives in Lafayette.

MR. SHUTE, an Evansville pioneer, taught a few children in his cabin as early as 1818, and in 1824, when the brick school-house was built, he was installed the village school-master.

Though not a teacher, WILLIAM MACLURE was, in an eminent degree, an educator in Indiana. He was born in Scotland in 1763, and died in Mexico in 1840. He acquired a fortune in business in early life, and then gave himself to the study of geology. He traveled extensively in the United States, and crossed the Alleghany mountains fifty times. In 1812, he assisted in organizing the Academy of Natural Sciences, at Philadelphia, of which he was elected president in 1817, and for every year thereafter until his death. He was an advocate of manual labor schools, one of which he attempted to establish in Spain, in 1819. This was a failure, involving great pecuniary loss. In 1824, he came to Indiana, and—in connection with *Thomas Say*, *Dr. Troost*, *Mr. Lesueur*, and others—attempted the same scheme at New Harmony. This, after a short, brilliant career, failed also, but it brought the Pestalozzian system of instruction into Indiana, and established, for many years, the great American geologist and the great American naturalist in this State. Here they pursued their studies and here their works were published. In his will Mr. Maclure made provision for the formation of "Working-men's Libraries." Large numbers of these were formed in various parts of Indiana.

THOMAS SAY lived at New Harmony while he pursued his studies and prepared for the publication of his works. He was born in Philadelphia in 1787, and was one of the founders of the Academy of Natural Sciences, in 1812. In 1815, he investigated the natural history of East Florida. In 1819, he went as naturalist with Long's expedition to the Rocky Mountains. In 1823, he accompanied the St. Peter's River Expedition in the same capacity. In 1825, he settled in New Harmony, and there spent the remainder of his life in the preparation of an American entomology, beautifully illustrated. The drawing, engraving, and coloring were all done at New Harmony. Mr. Say died October 10, 1834.

FRANCIS JOSEPH NICHOLAS NEEF, at the beginning of this century, was in the Army of the Rhine. In one of Napoleon's battles he received a musket ball, which he carried in his body till his death, in 1853. Soon after recovering from his wound, he became an assistant of Pestalozzi, in his school near Berne, in Switzerland. In 1803, he was sent by his principal to Paris, to introduce the Pestalozzian system in that city. In 1805, William Maclure visited Pestalozzi's school, and at once determined to have the system introduced into America. Accordingly, when he returned to Paris, he sent for Mr. Neef and said to him: "On what terms will you go to my country and introduce there your method of education? I have seen Pestalozzi. I know his system. My country wants it, and will receive it with enthusiasm. I engage to pay your passage and secure your livelihood. Go, and be your master's apostle in the new world." The result was that, in 1806, Mr. Neef came to America. He first established himself at the fords of the Schuylkill, near Philadelphia, on ground now within the limits of Fairmount Park, and here for many years he taught the Pestalozzian system. Many prominent men were trained in this school, among them the renowned Admiral Farragut. In 1808, he published his "Plan and Method of Education," and this was followed in 1813 by "The Methods of Teaching." Mr. Neef afterward went to Kentucky and from there, at the instance of Mr. Maclure, Thomas Say, Dr. Troost and others, came to New Harmony, where in 1826 he established another Pestalozzian school. The teachers in this school were, besides Mr. Neef, William Phiquepal, D'Arasmont (who was afterwards the husband of the celebrated Fanny Wright), Robert Dale Owen, and Mrs. Evans, a daughter of Mr. Neef.

This was the "Community School," but it was not

limited in its instruction to members of the Community. Many pupils came from other parts of the country to New Harmony, to secure its advantages. Higher institutions of learning were few in number and but poorly equipped. At that date, 1826, the State University had but one teacher, B. R. Hall. Hanover College had not yet assumed even the shape of Dr. Crowe's Grammar School. Wabash College, with its twelve students in the Preparatory Department, did not open for seven years, and Asbury University not until eleven years after the organization of this school. Here the Pestalozzian system was first taught in Indiana, and many young men went out from this school and taught the system in the rural districts and in the villages. After the breaking up of the Community, Mr. Neef went first to Cincinnati, afterwards to Steubenville, Ohio, and in 1835 he returned to New Harmony, where he passed the remaining eighteen years of his life.

MRS. FAUNTLEROY, a daughter of Robert Owen, and sister of Robert Dale Owen, afterwards taught some years in New Harmony. Prof. Richard Owen and J. Blackwood were lecturers in her school.

JUDGE WILLIAM A. PORTER was one of the early seminary teachers, having served several years as principal of the Harrison County Seminary at Corydon, Ind., commencing Jan., 1828. He graduated at Miami University, Sept. 26, 1827. After teaching a few years, he gave up that business and commenced the practice of law, which he still continues at Corydon.

REV. BYRAM LAWRENCE, a Baptist minister from Massachusetts, taught many years in the Clarke County

Seminary at Charlestown. He afterward went South and became a State geologist.

ISAAC McCOY, a native of Clarke County, and a graduate of Hanover College, was Mr. Lawrence's successor.

THOMAS HORNBROOK was born June 13, 1807, in Tavistock, Devonshire, England. He attended Eton Academy from his sixth to his eleventh year, and this completed his education; for at that time his father came to America, and settled in the wilds of Vanderburg County, Ind. He taught his first school in Princeton in 1830, and continued the profession some ten years in Gibson and Vanderburg Counties. He was three years principal of Gibson County Seminary. In 1850, he was admitted to practice at the bar. He served as Justice of the Peace, and was elected judge of the Vanderburg Court.

He died Dec. 8, 1855, at Union, Pike County, Ind.

SAMUEL R. CAVENS was one of the teachers in Monroe and Greene Counties, of men who are now sixty to seventy years of age. He taught in Bloomington more than fifty years ago. The author of "The New Purchase" compliments Mr. Cavens highly for his kindness of heart and for his musical talents, and assigns him the name of "Dan. Scrape" *the left-handed fiddler*. He was one of the best teachers of his time. He was afterwards elected to the office of Clerk of the Circuit Court, which office he filled with satisfaction to his constituents.

JUDGE WILLIAMSON DUNN, father of Hon. Wm. McKee Dunn, was born in Kentucky, in 1781. He settled in Crawfordsville, Ind., in 1824, at which time he was appointed Register in the Land Office by President Monroe. In 1832, he gave fifteen acres of land adjoining Crawfordsville to assist in establishing Wabash College. He also gave liberally to the establishment of Hanover College. He died at Hanover, in Jefferson County.

JAS. G. MAY, a native of Kentucky, emigrated to Indiana in 1824. After coming to Salem, he was under the instruction of John I. Morrison, but soon commenced teaching, first around Salem, then for five sessions as assistant to Mr. Morrison. From 1832 to 1834 he was editor of *The Western Annotator.* He was then principal of the Decatur County Seminary, at Greensburg, until 1839. During the next three years he practiced law. In 1843, he took charge of the Corydon High School, which he conducted for eight years, when he left to take charge of the New Albany schools, over which he presided for six years. In 1858, he again returned to Salem to take charge of the Washington County Seminary. This he conducted until 1871, when he was elected superintendent of the Salem Graded-Schools, from which position he retired in 1874. He is at present teaching private classes at his residence. Prof. May has had many pupils, who are to-day the living monuments of the faithful work of an instructor to whom no eulogy can do justice.

HARVEY NUTTING was born February 4, 1808, in Brimfield, Hampden County, Mass., and was educated in Wilbraham Academy. He came to Connersville, Indiana, July, 1832, and, opening a school in the county seminary the following month, he continued successfully therein for fifteen years. He also kept a private school for five years in Connersville, and taught ten years in Rush County, making in all thirty years of service as a teacher. Prof. Nutting is a man of fine talents and thorough education, and one of the best of classical scholars. Many of the leading men of the State received their education under his instruction. No man, perhaps, in the State has done more to advance local educational interests than he. Having by economy saved enough to enable him to live comfortably, he has retired from his profession, respected and revered by his former students and friends.

JAMES S. FERRIS was born September 14, 1818, in Franklin County, Indiana, and died at his residence in Winchester, September 22, 1870. He received his primary education at Brookville, and with William Haughton in Union County. He commenced teaching at seventeen. In 1839, he removed to Winchester and took charge of the county seminary, which he made a popular school for eight years. He was married December 8, 1844, to Miss Mary Hull. In 1847, he removed to Muncie and took charge of the seminary there for three years, when he removed to New Castle and took charge of the seminary for five years in connection with Rev. R. B. Abbot. In New Castle he was also Deputy County Treasurer, and was elected to the State Legislature for one term. In 1855, he was elected Auditor of Henry County, which position he held for eight years. He next moved to Muncie in 1863, and to Iowa in 1865. He, however, returned to Winchester in 1866, and settled there as superintendent of the graded-schools, where he remained until his decease. He was a consistent Christian, and was licensed to preach in his twenty-third year. His teaching was a labor of love, and bore fruit in the characters of the students that placed themselves under his tuition. With him, kindness and firmness were so blended as to command the universal esteem of patron and pupil.

Z. B. Sturgus was educated at Salem, Indiana, and at Hanover College. He taught at the former place with Hon. John I. Morrison, and after graduating at Hanover went to Charlestown, Clarke County, and there remained and taught a classical school some eighteen years. After losing his hearing, Mr. Sturgus gave up teaching and accepted a clerkship in the Department of the Interior, at Washington, D. C., where he is at present.

Rev. Martin M. Post was born December 3, 1805, in Cornwall, Vermont. His father, Martin Post, was a lawyer in Middlebury, Vermont. Mr. Post graduated from Middlebury College in 1826, and from Andover Theological Seminary in 1829. In the fall of the same year he emigrated to Indiana and located at Logansport, where he organized a Presbyterian church, and was its pastor forty years. He first taught in Indiana in 1838–9, and was principal of the Cass County Seminary from 1849 to 1854.

Mrs. Lucretia H. Post, wife of the above, was also one of the early teachers of Logansport, having taught there as early as 1833.

Among the early school-masters of Logansport the following may be mentioned: John McKinney, 1828–9; George Lyon, 1829–31; Rev. H. A. Hunter, 1830–1; Mrs. John B. Turner, 1829–31; Thomas J. Wilson, 1831; Selba Harney, 1832.

Cornelius Pering was born in 1806, in England. After teaching a short time in his native country, he emigrated to America in 1832; located in Bloomington, Indiana, and took charge of the Monroe County Female Academy. He presided over this school until 1848, when he went to Louisville, where he took a private school, in which he continued twenty-six years. In 1874 he returned to Europe, and now makes his home in London.

RAWSON VAILE was born May 28, 1812, in Winhall, Bennington County, Vt. He was educated in the common schools of Vermont, at Amherst Academy, and at Amherst College, Massachusetts, from which he graduated in 1839. Having taught three years in Massachusetts, in 1840 he removed to Indiana, and opened a school at Richmond, Wayne County. The writer, though a boy at the time, recollects well Mr. Vaile as an active worker in an Educational Convention, held in Richmond in 1840—the first convention of the kind in the State. After two years, Mr. Vaile removed to Centreville to take charge of the Wayne County Seminary, which he conducted until 1848. His labors as teacher ended here, but, after his removal to Kokomo, Howard County, his present residence, he was for a number of years County Examiner. He has always taken an intelligent and hearty interest in the success of the public schools.

RUFUS PATCH was born April 16, 1819, in Groton, Mass. He graduated at Western Reserve College in 1841, and studied theology in Lane Theological Seminary. In 1844, he took charge of Lagrange Collegiate Institute, and has retained that position twenty-two years out of the thirty-two that have since passed. He still labors in the same position. Mr. Patch was an active member of the Northern Indiana Teachers' Institute from 1849 to 1854, and was at one time its President. In 1854, he assisted in organizing the Indiana State Teachers' Association. A catalogue of the Lagrange Collegiate Institute, recently published, gives the number of pupils, during Mr. Patch's administration, as 1471, of which 859 were gentleman and 612 ladies. Many of these are now prominent lawyers, physicians, teachers, ministers, farmers, merchants, etc.

REV. EBENEZER TUCKER is a man so modest that he would not knowingly give any information of himself that could be wrought into a sketch. The writer has seen more or less of his worth for thirty years, and knows with what patient, Christian love he has labored for the elevation of the poor and ignorant. He was educated at Whitesboro, N. Y., and at Oberlin College. In 1846, he was selected as principal of Union Literary Institute, a manual labor school for colored people, located in Randolph County, Ind. Under discouragements that would sink any heart, not constrained by the love of God, he labored for ten years. Thinking then that he should do something for his growing family, he removed to Jo Daviess County, Ill. In 1859, he was recalled to Indiana to take charge of Liber College, in Jay County. This school was opened in 1853, by Rev. I. N. Taylor, who continued in it until Mr. Tucker took charge. Here, under the excellent instruction of these two gentlemen, hundreds of the youth of Jay County were led up to and through the higher branches of knowledge, and scores of young men and women have been prepared to become teachers. Mr. Tucker next took charge of the schools of Union City, then of a college for colored people in New Orleans. After spending several years in faithful labor there and in Hinds County, Miss., he returned to Indiana, and has for the past two years been laboring at the head of Union Literary Institute, his first love in this State.

Mr. Tucker has few or no superiors as a teacher.

E. P. COLE, A. M., was born at Bergen, N. J., and graduated at Miami University. He taught ten years in Ohio, and then came in 1849 to Indiana, and took charge of Randolph County Seminary. In 1853, at the organization of the public schools of Indianapolis, Mr. Cole was made principal of the High School. The next year he took an active part in the organization of the Indiana State Teachers' Association, and in 1855 he presented a report to that body which resulted in the establishment of the *Indiana School Journal.* As an agent for the association he canvassed a large part of the State, obtaining subscribers for the *Journal,* and lecturing upon educational topics. In 1857, he took charge of Monroe County Female Seminary, in which position he served till 1863. During this period he was one of the School Examiners, and, as such, managed the first Teachers' Institute ever held in the county. He has since been superintendent of schools at Wabash, Bloomington, Greencastle, and Washington. During the past two years, Mr. Cole has had charge of Hopewell Academy, near Franklin, in Johnson County.

COLLEGE FACULTIES.

ANDREW WYLIE, D.D., first president of Indiana State University, was born April 12, 1789, in Fayette County, Penn. His parents came from Ireland about the beginning of the Revolutionary War. He received his early instruction from his mother. He supported himself while in college, and graduated with the first honor at Canonsburgh, Penn., in 1810. After serving one year as tutor in the same institution, he was unanimously elected its president. In this position he served till 1817, when he accepted the presidency of Washington College, only seven miles from Canonsburgh, hoping that he would be enabled to unite the two. In this, however, he did not succeed. In 1828, he was called to Indiana to take charge as president of the *Indiana College.* Here he performed the great work of his life, and though he was often opposed in his plans, sometimes by members of the faculty, his work stood the test of critical investigation. Twenty-two classes, including one hundred and forty young men, graduated at the State University under President Wylie, and large numbers of others were there, under his instructions, for a partial course. Many of his students have become eminent men, some as missionaries in foreign lands, others as ministers in our own land, and others as members of Congress, supreme judges, professors in colleges, and in numerous other positions of honor and trust. His baccalaureates and other addresses were of a high order. His eulogy on Lafayette elicited a letter from Daniel Webster, in which he spoke of the production in the highest terms. He published several small works and numerous addresses, and left two manuscripts—one on the training of youth, and the other on rhetoric. He died at Bloomington, November 11, 1851, and a monument to his memory was erected by the students of the University and the citizens of the town.

William M. Daily, D.D., LL.D., was educated at Indiana State University, where he graduated in 1836.

He commenced preaching before he graduated. In 1849, he was elected professor of elocution in St. Charles College, Mo. From 1853 to 1859, he was president of the Indiana State University. Since the war he has been doing missionary work among the freedmen in Louisiana.

CYRUS NUTT, D.D., LL.D., was born in Trumbull County, Ohio, 1814. His early education was received from his parents and from an occasional three months' school. At the age of eighteen he commenced preparing for college. After graduating at Meadville, Pa., he taught six months in the preparatory department of the same institution, and was then elected to take charge of the preparatory department of Indiana Asbury University. He traveled by steamboat and stage from Meadville to Putnamville, Indiana, and thence on foot to Greencastle. In June, 1837, he commenced the work of opening this new institution in a small room of a one-story brick building. He remained in connection with this institution as professor of languages six years, and afterwards returned in 1848 for one year, and again in 1857 for three years. He was also president of the Fort Wayne College one year, and of Whitewater College five years. During the last fifteen years of his life he was president of the Indiana University at Bloomington. He was a member of the Indiana State Teachers' Association from its organization in 1854. In 1861, he was elected president of that body. He was a valuable member of the State Board of Education. He died at Bloomington, Indiana, August, 1875.

LEMUEL MOSS, D.D., president of Indiana State University, was born in Boone County, Kentucky, in

1829, and removed to Dearborn County, Indiana, when he was four years old. At the age of fifteen he entered the office of the *Lawrenceburg Register*, as type-setter. During the next nine years he worked in the printing-offices of Cincinnati, and for a time was foreman of the stereotype establishment of J. A. & U. P. James. At the age of twenty-two he married Miss Harriet Bingham, of Zanesville, Ohio, and two years after (1853) commenced his college course in the university at Rochester, N. Y. He graduated from this institution at the age of twenty-eight, and from the theological seminary at the age of thirty. The same year, 1860, he commenced preaching in Worcester, Mass. During the war he was Home Secretary of the Christian Commission. In 1865, he was elected professor of theology in the University at Lewisburg, Pa. From 1868 to 1872, he was editor of the *National Baptist*, published in Philadelphia. In 1872, he held a professorship in Crozer Theological Seminary. In 1874, he was made president of the University of Chicago, and in 1875 he became the president of the Indiana State University.

Daniel Read, LL.D., was Professor of Ancient Languages in Indiana State University from 1843 to 1856, and as such gave instruction to many who are prominent men in this and other states. In 1851 a new constitution was to be formed for Indiana, and Prof. Read was sent as a delegate to the convention to represent Monroe County. At the organization of a normal department in the State University, Mr. Read was placed at its head. In 1856 he was elected to a professorship in Wisconsin University, and afterwards to the presidency of Missouri University, which position he still retains.

DANIEL KIRKWOOD, LL.D., was a son of John and Agnes Kirkwood, and was born, in 1814, in Hartford County, Maryland. At the age of twenty he entered the Academy at York, Penn., where he remained nine years, part of the time as pupil and the remainder as teacher of mathematics. In 1843, he was called by Col. John W. Forney and Hon. Thaddeus Stevens, directors of Lancaster city schools, to the principalship of the Lancaster High School. He early gave attention to the subject of astronomy, and in 1849 published his celebrated Analogy. This and subsequent papers, prepared by Prof. Kirkwood, soon gave him a world-wide reputation among astronomers. In 1851 he was called to the chair of Mathematics in Delaware College. In 1856, he came to Indiana as Professor of Mathematics in the State University, in which position he is serving at this time. For several years he was editor of the mathematical department of the Indiana School Journal. His style of writing is concise. He has been a frequent contributor to various scientific journals, and his articles have been copied on both sides of the Atlantic. He has published two works on astronomy, in one of which he made predictions in regard to the *lost comet,* which subsequent observations have verified.

PROF. RICHARD OWEN, son of Robert Owen, was born at New Lanark, Scotland, 1810, and was educated at Hofwyl, in Switzerland. He came to Indiana, in 1828. He taught three years in New Harmony, served a year and a half as captain in the Mexican War, assisted his brother David Dale Owen in the Geological

Survey of the North-west, served as professor in the Western Military Institute, six years in Kentucky and three and a half in Tennessee, in which position he was associated with Hon. J. G. Blaine. He served as State Geologist of Indiana in 1859 and '60. In 1861, he became Lieutenant-colonel of the 15th Indiana Infantry, and, after the battle of Greenbrier, was promoted to a Colonelcy. In 1862, he took charge of 4,000 prisoners, captured at Fort Donelson and detained at Camp Morton, and his treatment of them was such that when he was himself made prisoner at Mumfordsville, he was released without parole and his side-arms were returned to him. He was with Grant at the capture of Vicksburg and with Banks in the Red River Expedition. Since 1863, he has worthily filled the chair of Natural Science in Indiana State University.

DR. JOHN FINLEY CROWE, the founder of Hanover College, was born at Greenville, Tenn., 1789. He pursued his collegiate studies at Transylvania University, and his theological studies at Princeton. He conducted a female seminary for a time, at Shelbyville, Ky. In 1822, he came to Indiana on the invitation of the church at Hanover, and in 1827 opened a grammar school at that place. This grew in numbers and influence until 1833, when it was chartered as Hanover College. To this institution Dr. Crowe devoted the remainder of his life. Many were the trials through which he passed, but his cheerful faith, indomitable energy, and untiring perseverance, were equal to every emergency, and he lived to see the harvest of his sowing, in the ministerial services of his own sons, and of others who graduated at this institution.

He was more than the professor, more than the president—he was the founder and father of the college. His death occurred at Hanover, in December, 1860.

REV. SYLVESTER SCOVEL, D. D., was born March 3, 1796, in Peru, Berkshire County, Mass. After a four years' course he graduated at William's College, Massachusetts, in 1822, and at Princeton (N. J.) Theological Seminary, in 1825. He removed to Indiana in 1829, laboring in Harrison, Ohio, and Dearborn County for ten years. In 1836, he became agent in the West of the Board of Domestic Missions, in which work he continued for ten years with remarkable energy and success. In 1846, Dr. Scovel was elected president of Hanover College. He died suddenly of cholera, July 4, 1849, in the midst of eminently successful labor.

DR. THOMAS E. THOMAS, chosen president of Hanover College after the death of Dr. Scovel, delivered his inaugural address in March, 1850, and continued at the head of the institution for five years. He was born at Chelmsford, Essex, in England, in 1812. The family, emigrating to America, came to Cincinnati in 1818. Dr. Thomas received his early education, and only college preparation from his father and mother, and graduated at Miami University in 1834. The then president of Miami was Dr. Bishop, for whom his pupil had the greatest love and reverence, and who exerted the chiefest influence on his subsequent life and character. After teaching first at Rising Sun, Ind., then at Harrison, and Franklin in Ohio, he became, in 1838, the pastor of the Presbyterian Church at Hamilton, Ohio, where he was still engaged when chosen to the presidency of Hanover College twelve years afterward. Dr. Thomas resigned his position in the college in 1854, to accept the chair of Biblical

Literature and Exegesis in the New Albany Theological Seminary. These duties he discharged, till, four years afterwards, the seminary was removed to Chicago. Remaining in New Albany a time as stated supply to the Banks Street Presbyterian Church there, he accepted a call to the First Presbyterian Church of Dayton, Ohio, where he continued to preach for about thirteen years. In 1871, he was elected to, and accepted the chair of New Testament Greek and Exegesis in Lane Theological Seminary at Walnut Hills, Ohio.

In the fourth year of his labors there, he died of pleuro-pneumonia, February 2, 1875.

Dr. Thomas was a man possessed of a retentive memory, persistent industry, accurate and varied scholarship, great zeal in the cause of education, and justly deserved fame as an extempore speaker and pulpit orator. With no branch of learning taught in our colleges did he lack a scholarly acquaintance, except perhaps that of Modern Languages. Rev. S. F. Scovel, D. D., son of a former president of Hanover, now of Pittsburgh, Pa., thus writes: "As a teacher, Dr. Thomas was unsurpassed. He passed easily from department to department, appreciating thorough work, and detecting shams every-where. His method was varied, but always intelligible. Adhering to the text-book, it was only as the body adheres to the spinal column. He built up upon text-books the thoughts and feelings of the whole subject. No question ever found him off his guard, and none ever frightened him into an unwary decision or harsh reproof. . . . . As president, he came to a most difficult task, and never shrank from toil in accomplishing it. The financial question pressed all the time, in the form of supplying salaries from an inadequate fund, and urging a half-interested and struggling church to the work of building and endowment. Along with this, Dr. Thomas entered quite as vigorously upon efforts to uplift the standard of scholarship, to improve the methods of teaching, to increase the library, apparatus, and cabinets. All the success possible under the circumstances was won."

When Dr. Thomas took charge of Hanover College, the number of students was about 150; the total endowment, $30,000; his salary, as president, $800, and that of the professors, $600 each. It had been chartered and in operation as a college fifteen years.

The efforts of Dr. Thomas and his colleagues for the success of the college were not unrewarded. There was awakened an ambition and tone of scholarship which will be remembered by the students of those days with pride. The number in attendance increased each year—during the last year of his presidency it was 203.

Rev. Geo. C. Heckman, D. D., was born at Easton, Pa., January 26, 1825. He received his preparatory training in the academy of Rev. John Van Dervear, D. D., at Easton, entering Lafayette College, Pennsylvania, in 1841. He graduated in 1845, and entered the Theological Seminary at Princeton, N. J., from which he graduated in 1848. He was pastor of various Presbyterian churches in New York, Wisconsin, and Indiana, until 1870, when he was called to the presidency of Hanover College, Indiana, where he still remains.

Elihu W. Baldwin, D. D., the first president of

Wabash College, was born December 25, 1789, in Durham, N. Y. He was a graduate of Yale College of the class of 1812, and of Andover Theological Seminary of the class of 1817. He became pastor of the Seventh Presbyterian Church in New York City, December 25, 1820, and was elected to the presidency of Wabash College in February, 1835. He died October 15th, 1840. As president of the college he was deservedly and universally popular; as a teacher and lecturer his talents were of a high order; as a disciplinarian he was mild and paternal; as a preacher of the gospel he was uncommonly successful. In all the various relations he sustained to the church and the commonwealth at large, Dr. Baldwin acted well his part, and impressed the influence of a noble character upon his age.

CHARLES WHITE, D. D., second president of Wabash College, was born 1795, at Randolph Mass. He was a lineal descendant of the Pilgrims. He graduated with first honors at Dartmouth College in 1812, and pursued his theological studies at Andover. From 1825 to 1841, he preached at Thetford, Vt., Cazenovia, and Oswego, N. Y. In 1841, he accepted the presidency of Wabash College at Crawfordsville, Ind., in which position he served acceptably during the remainder of his life.

He published a number of sermons, addresses, essays, etc., besides a volume of nearly 500 pages. He died suddenly, October 29th, 1861.

JOSEPH F. TUTTLE, D.D., third president of Wabash College, was the son of Rev. Jacob Tuttle, and was born in New Jersey, 1818. He received his early education at Newark Academy and at Granville, Ohio;

graduated with first honors at Marietta College in 1841; the same year he entered Lane Theological Seminary. He preached two years at Delaware, Ohio, and fifteen years at Rockaway, N. J. In 1862 he was called to the presidency of Wabash College. In this position he has now been fourteen years, doing valuable service for the cause of education. Dr. Tuttle's sermons at home and abroad, his chapel lectures, and his many addresses before lyceums and literary societies, have all been of an elevated character, and are deservedly popular.

John L. Campbell, LL.D., the *projector of the Centennial celebration and National Exposition*, was born at Salem, Washington County, Indiana. His early education was received in Salem Academy. In 1848, he graduated at Wabash College, and about a year afterwards was appointed tutor in the same institution. In 1851, he became principal of the preparatory department. In 1854, he was elected Professor of Mathematics, Natural Philosophy, and Astronomy. This position he still holds. In 1864, he delivered an address at the Smithsonian Institute on the life and teachings of Galileo. The occasion of this address was the completion of the third century since the birth of the great philosopher. This occasion suggested to Prof. Campbell the idea of holding the International Exposition and Centennial Celebration of 1876 at Philadelphia. In 1866, he addressed letters to Hon. Henry S. Lane, U. S. Senator, and Hon. Morton McMichael, mayor of Philadelphia, on the subject. The initiatory steps were taken, and the Centennial Commission was organized with Prof. Campbell as a prominent member. Since 1873 he has held the office of Permanent Secretary of the Commission, and has labored almost incessantly for the success of the enterprise.

BISHOP MATTHEW SIMPSON, the first president of Indiana Asbury University, was born in Cadiz, Ohio. He was educated in the common schools at home, and at Connellsville, Pa. He studied medicine, and for a while practiced it. In 1839, he was Professor of Natural Science and Mathematics in Alleghany College, when he was elected to the presidency of Indiana Asbury University, which position he filled with remarkable success until 1848. He then removed to Cincinnati and edited the *Western Christian Advocate* until 1852, when he was elected Bishop of the M. E. Church. As president, his influence over the students was almost unbounded. They loved him, and do we not serve whom we love? In the pulpit his voice is soft and full of entreaty, and receives its authority from the love he bears to God, rather than from the schools of men.

L. W. BERRY, D.D., of whom the writer can learn little, was elected the second president of Asbury University in 1849. In 1855, he was elected president of Iowa Wesleyan University. He died in July, 1858.

DANIEL CURRY, D.D., was born November 26, 1809, in Peekskill, N. Y. He graduated at the Wesleyan University in 1827; was Professor of Greek in Georgia Female College in 1839; was elected president of Indiana Asbury University in 1854, and served three years in this capacity. He edited Southey's Life of Wesley, and a Life of Wicliffe.

BISHOP THOMAS BOWMAN was born in Pennsylvania, 1817. He obtained his education at Wilbraham, Mass., Cazenovia, N. Y., and Dickinson College, Carlisle, Penn. At the last named institution he graduated in 1837. After studying law one year, he gave it up in the spring of 1839 and commenced preaching. In 1840, he took charge of the Grammar School of Dickinson College. In 1848, he organized Dickinson Seminary at Williamsport, Penn., where he remained ten years. In 1858, he was called to the presidency of Indiana Asbury University. He was a successful and popular president. He was elected chaplain of the U. S. Senate in 1864, and in 1872 the General Conference elected him to the responsible office of Bishop of the Methodist Church. His residence since that time has been in St. Louis, Mo.

REUBEN ANDRUS, LL.D., was born in Jefferson County, New York, in 1824. His early life was spent upon a farm in Fulton County, Ill. At the age of twenty-one he entered the preparatory department of Illinois College at Jacksonville. Having no means, he worked his way through college in five years, and at once entered the ministry. In 1866, he organized Quincy College, but remained in charge of it only one year. In 1872, he was called to the presidency of Asbury University, which position he filled with ability three years.

ALEXANDER MARTIN, D. D., son of James Martin and Janet Urquhart, was born January 24, 1824, in Nairnshire, Scotland. He graduated from Alleghany College in 1847, in which institution he served ten years as professor of Greek. In 1867, he was elected first president of West Virginia University, in which position he served until 1875, when he was elected president of Indiana Asbury University. This position he now holds.

SILAS BAILEY, D. D., was born in Worcester County, Mass., June 12, 1809, and died in Paris, France, June 30, 1874.

He lived on a farm until he was nineteen years old, when he went to Amherst, Mass., and prepared for college. He entered Brown University in 1830, and remained till the spring of 1834, when he left college, and took charge of Worcester Academy. About 1839, he commenced preaching in Thompson, Conn. In 1847, he went to Granville, Ohio, as president of Granville College. In 1852, he became president of Franklin College at Franklin, Indiana, in which capacity he labored faithfully for ten years, when his health failed, and he was compelled to give up teaching.

After a few years rest at Lafayette, he again attempted to teach as professor of metaphysics in Kalamazoo College, Michigan. He remained there but a short time. In 1873, he went to France, where he survived only a few months. His large library, and the most of his property, he left to Franklin College.

W. T. STOTT, was born May 22, 1836, in Jennings County, Ind. In his fifteenth year he was sent to Sardinia Academy, where he studied for three years. In 1856, he entered Franklin College, where he graduated in 1861. In August, of the same year, he joined the 18th Indiana Volunteer Infantry, in which he served two years as private and two years as captain of the company in which he enlisted, commanding his regiment in the battle of Cedar Creek. In 1865, he entered Rochester Theological Seminary, from which he graduated in 1868. In 1869, he accepted the chair of Natural Science in Franklin College. In 1872, he spent a few months teaching in Kalamazoo College, Michigan, and in the same year was called to the presidency of Franklin College, which position he now fills.

REUBEN D. ROBINSON, D. D. was born near Urbana, O., in 1818, and was educated at Indiana Asbury University, graduating in 1843. Two years later, he entered the Northern Indiana Conference. His educational work has been in connection with the For Wayne College, of which he has been president nearly twenty years.

OTHER PRESIDENTS OF FORT WAYNE COLLEGE were A. C. Huestis, Rev. G. M. Round, Rev. C. Nutt, Rev. Samuel T. Gillett, Rev. Samuel Brenton, Rev. F. M. Heminway, and Rev. J. B. Robinson.

THOMAS HARRISON was born in England, 1813, where he received an academic education. He came to America in 1835. As associate publisher of the Springfield Ohio Pioneer and assistant editor of the Western Christian Advocate, he spent his time till 1848. Since 1849, he has devoted his energies to teaching. He was eight years at Linden Hill Academy, New Carlisle, O., and six years president of Moore's Hill College, Indiana. He has also taught at Brookville and some other places, and for several years past has been principal of Shelbyville High School. He is the author of the numeral system of musical notation, in which several books have been published by himself and others. He is also the author of a work on elocution.

ALLEN R. BENTON was born October 1, 1822, in Cayuga County, N. Y. In 1843, he entered Fulton

Academy, and in 1845, Bethany College, Virginia, Alexander Campbell, president. From here he graduated with honors as Bachelor of Arts in 1847. In 1848, he became principal of Farmers Academy, Rush County, Ind. In 1855, he accepted the professorship of Languages in the North-western Christian University at Indianapolis, and in 1861 the presidency of the same. The next three years he was professor and president of Alliance College, Ohio, and was then elected chancellor of the University of Nebraska at Lincoln, which position he still occupies. Having been lately elected to a professorship in the North-western Christian University, he has signified his intention to accept and return to the field of his former labors at Indianapolis. It may be truly said of President Benton that he bends all his energies to the success of his work, whether at the head of an institution or in one of its chairs. He is truly ranked with the first educators of his day.

OTIS A. BURGESS was born August 26, 1829, in Thompson, Windham County, Conn. His opportunities for education were poor until he was seventeen, when he entered Norwich Academy, N. Y. He remained here but a short time, and then left to teach his first school. At the age of eighteen, he emigrated to Woodford County, Ill., where he taught during the four following years. He then resolved to prepare for the pulpit. For this purpose he entered Bethany College, Virginia, and studied under Alexander Campbell. In 1854, he graduated and received the degree of A. B. He returned to Illinois, and was one year acting-president of Eureka College. Since that time his labors have been divided between the pulpit and the professor's chair, in both of which he has had constant success.

In 1868, he became president of the North-western Christian University, in which position he has continued until this time, excepting a two years' absence in Chicago, as pastor of a congregation of the Christian Church.

NICHOLAS SUMMERBELL was born March 8th, 1816, at Peekskill, N. Y. Of his education the writer has no data. In 1859, he was elected the first president of Union Christian College at Merom, Ind., over which he presided for six years, gaining and keeping the love and confidence of the students and friends of the institution. He resigned to return to the ministry in 1865, leaving the college with full classes and clear of liabilities.

Dr. Summerbell is better known as a preacher, debater, author, and champion of his adopted Christian Church than as a teacher.

THOMAS HOLMES, D. D., second president of Union Christian College, was born November 24, 1817, in the town of Royalton, N. Y. His life from 1835 to 1843, was one of alternate teaching and preparation for college. He entered Oberlin in 1843, and graduated in 1847. In 1853, he commenced service as Professor of Greek in Antioch College, Ohio. In 1855, having leave of absence, he sailed for Europe, to continue the study of Greek in the German Universities at Bonn, Berlin, and Geneva. He returned in 1857, and was pastor of churches, successively, in Portsmouth, N. H., Fall River, Mass., Schoharie, N. Y., from 1857 to 1865, when he was called to the presidency of Union Christian College, at Merom, Ind., which position he held until 1875, when he resigned and removed to Ann Arbor, Mich.

LETTICE SMITH HOLMES wife of the above, and nine years professor of German, French, and Latin, in Union Christian College, was born May 8, 1823. In addition to her thorough education at Oberlin, she went to Europe and continued her studies with her husband.

WILLIAM A. JONES, A. M., PRESIDENT OF INDIANA STATE NORMAL SCHOOL was born in Middlesex County, Conn., 1830. His education was obtained in the common schools of his native State and at Williston Seminary, in Massachusetts. He taught district school in Bristol, Conn., and "boarded round." He served three years as secretary and treasurer of a manufacturing establishment. In 1856, he went to Illinois. He taught seven years at Altona and was six years superintendent of schools at Aurora. In 1870, he was elected president of the Indiana State Normal School at Terre Haute, which position he accepted, and commenced at once the work of organizing that institution. He has been eminently successful in bringing this young institution up to the standard of the best Normal Schools in this country.

Mr. Jones is also a working member of the State Board of Education and a valuable addition to the State Teachers' Association.

JOSEPH MOORE, A. M., was born in 1832, in Washington County, Ind. His early education was obtained mostly in the public schools, until he was eighteen years of age, when he commenced to teach. In 1853, at the age of twenty-one, he entered as a pupil in the Friends' Boarding School at Richmond, Ind. The next year he was employed in the same as a teacher, continuing until 1859, when he entered Harvard University. In this institution he spent two years in the study of chemistry, botany, and comparative anatomy, under Professors Horsford, Gray, and Wyman. He was also greatly benefited by attending the lectures of Prof. Agassiz. Here he received the degree of Bachelor of Science. In 1862, he became professor of chemistry and botany in Earlham College. In 1868, the honorary degree of A. M., was conferred on him by Haverford College, of Pennsylvania. In 1869, he was made president of Earlham College, which position he has held to the present time.

The principal service he has rendered to education, besides teaching, has been the collection of the Earlham Cabinet of Natural History, which has received important additions the past year by his visit to the Sandwich Islands. Joseph Moore is loved and respected by all who know him either as a friend, a teacher, a citizen, a lecturer, or as a minister of the gospel.

A. C. SHORTRIDGE was born October 22, 1833, in Henry County, Indiana. He was educated at Fairview, Rush County, and at Green Mount, near Richmond. He taught three years at Milton and Dublin; was then made Professor of Mathematics at Whitewater College, which institution he leased in 1856, conducting it for five years. Prof. Shortridge was one of the Wayne County teachers who in 1854 assisted in organizing the Indiana State Teachers' Association. He has attended every annual meeting of that body for the past twenty-one years. In 1863, he was called to superintend the Indianapolis schools, which he organized and brought up to the standard of the best in the West. In 1874, after eleven years' successful service, he resigned to accept the presidency of Purdue University. This position he has just resigned, and is now a resident of Indianapolis. He has been connected as publisher or associate editor with the *Little Chief*, the *Indiana Teacher*, the *Educationist*, and the *Indiana School Journal.*

SARAH ALLEN OREN is a native of Clinton County, Ohio, and was educated at Antioch College while Horace Mann was president. She came to Indiana in 1868, since which time she has been a teacher, except the two years while she was State Librarian. At this time she occupies the chair of Botany in Purdue University.

LEWIS PRUGH was born March 5, 1840, in Madison County, Ohio. When fifteen years of age, he entered the preparatory department of Antioch College, from which he graduated in 1861. The next year he taught in the Old Academy, at Merom, Ind. In 1862, he was Professor of Latin in Antioch College. In 1866, he was principal of East Hamburg Academy, near Buffalo. In 1869, he took charge of the graded-school at Fort Branch, Ind., and in 1872 he was elected president of Vincennes University, which position he still holds.

RYLAND T. BROWN was born in Mason County, Kentucky, October, 1807, and was educated in the common schools of Clermont County, Ohio, until his fourteenth year. He removed to Rush County, Indiana, in 1821, and commenced teaching in the common schools in 1826. During his leisure hours he pursued the study of medicine, and attended the sessions of the Ohio Medical College of 1827–8 and 1828–9, at the close of which he received the degree of M. D. In 1830, he located as physician in Connersville, and continued the study of Natural Science, teaching classes in chemistry in the winter, and botany in the spring. In 1844, he moved to Crawfordsville. At this time he began the special study of geology, and the examination of the adjacent coal-fields. Wabash College conferred on him the honorary degree of A.M. in 1850. He was appointed State Geologist by Gov. Wright in 1854, and Professor of Natural Science in the Northwestern Christian University in 1858, in which capacity he served thirteen years. In 1871, he was appointed Chemist-in-Chief of the Department of Agriculture at Washington, D. C. The following year he published his Physiology and Hygiene. In 1873, he resigned his position, returned to Indiana, and received his appointment of Professor of Physiology in the medical department of the Indiana State University, of which department he is now president.

SUPERINTENDENTS OF PUBLIC INSTRUCTION.

HON. WILLIAM C. LARRABEE was born at Cape Elizabeth, Maine, in 1802. He obtained his education through difficulties, and graduated at Bowdoin College, 1828. He taught two years at Alfred, Me., one year at Middletown, Conn., and then became principal of the Oneida Conference Seminary at Cazenovia, N. Y., where he did valuable service, educating seven who were afterwards presidents of colleges, twenty-seven principals of seminaries, and twelve editors of religious periodicals. Among these may be mentioned Dr. Tefft, Bishop Bowman, and P. B. Wilber. In 1835, he returned to Maine to take charge of the Maine Wesleyan Seminary, where his success was as eminent as it had been at Cazenovia. In 1841, he came to Indiana as a professor in Asbury University. While in that position he wrote and published several works, and was a regular contributor to the *Ladies' Repository*. In 1852, he was elected first Superintendent of Public Instruction. In 1854, he was defeated in the canvass for a second term, but was elected again in 1856. He retired from office in January, 1859, and died the following May.

HON. CALEB MILLS, the second Superintendent of Public Instruction for Indiana, was born in Dunbarton, New Hampshire, July 29, 1806. He graduated at Dartmouth College, 1828, and afterwards attended Andover Theological Seminary. In 1833, he accepted the position of principal of a preparatory school at Crawfordsville, which afterwards ripened into Wabash College. He was chosen Professor of Greek Language and Literature, a position he has eminently filled most of the time since. Prof. Mills was author of a series of valuable papers, whose object was to arouse the people of the State to a realization of their educational needs. These papers were published as "An Address to the Legislature." The agitation resulted in a vote by the people of the State in 1848 in favor of free schools.

In 1854, Prof. Mills was elected Superintendent of Public Instruction. During his official term of two years and three months he made three reports, in which were elaborately discussed many topics of vital importance to the success of the public school system. After his term of office expired, he returned to his professorship in Wabash College, where he is still connected.

HON. SAMUEL L. RUGG was born in 1805, in Oneida County, N. Y. Of his education, the writer has no account. He removed to Indiana about 1836, and took a prominent part in improvements in Adams County, where he resided. He was principal proprietor of Decatur, its county seat. He represented Allen and Adams Counties in the State Senate. He was Superintendent of Public Instruction for the State from 1859 to 1861, and from 1863 to 1865. Near the close of his last term, he united very cordially with his successor in efforts to increase the usefulness of the school system by securing proper legislation. In the performance of his duties as officer, he gave general satisfaction. He died on the 28th of March, 1871, in Nashville, Tenn., after a protracted illness.

HON. MILES J. FLETCHER was born in 1828, in Indianapolis. He graduated in 1852, at Brown University, Providence, R. I., and at once took position as professor of English Literature in Indiana Asbury University at Greencastle. After eight years service in this position, he was elected in 1860 to the office of Superintendent of Public Instruction. He entered upon his duties with that enthusiasm for which he was noted, and bade fair to do much valuable work; but during the civil war he was called away much of his time to assist in organizing the regiments that were preparing for the field. He was killed in a railroad accident, May 10, 1862, while on an errand of mercy to sick and wounded soldiers.

HON. SAM'L K. HOSHOUR, A. M., was born Dec. 9, 1803, in York County, Pa. With work in summer and school in winter, time passed until his seventeenth year, with little desire for mental improvement. At this time, however, he was called into service as a country school-master. This position aroused him, and so increased his thirst for an education, that he placed himself under the supervision of Dr. J. G. Schmucker, of York, Pa. In 1824, he was transferred to a theological institution at New Market, Va., under the instruction of Prof. S. S. Schmucker, and two years afterwards attained his first pastoral charge. Having emigrated to Indiana in 1835, he was tendered the supervision of the Wayne County Seminary at Centerville, which was accepted. He continued here three years as teacher and preacher, when he accepted the principalship of the Cambridge City Seminary, where he continued seven years. In Wayne County, he is remembered as one of the faithful and efficient teachers.

In 1855, he was elected president of the North-western Christian University at Indianapolis, but at the end of three years he became, from choice, professor of Modern Languages. In 1862, after the death of Superintendent M. J. Fletcher, Prof. Hoshour was appointed to fill the unexpired term. Prof. Hoshour has just been made glad by his friends, parishioners, and former pupils in their hearty celebration of his golden wedding.

HON. GEORGE W. HOSS, LL. D., was a native of Ohio. He came to Indiana in 1836, and worked on a farm till 1845, when he entered college at Greencastle, where he graduated in 1850—having in the mean-time earned his support, partly by teaching three hours per day in a female seminary. Since that time, he has been constantly in the educational work. He spent two years at Muncie, twelve years at Indianapolis in the Institute for the Blind, the Indiana Female College, the North-western Christian University, and as superintendent of the city schools. In 1864, he was elected superintendent of Public Instruction for the State, and was re-elected in 1866. During his two terms of office he aided in securing the passage of the Normal School bill and the re-enactment of the law permitting local taxation for the support of public schools. In 1868, he was elected professor of English Literature in the State University, which position he has retained ever since, except for an interval of two years while he was president of the Kansas State Normal School. Prof. Hoss was one of the pioneer institute workers in Indiana, and in this field has done much valuable work. He has been an active member of the State Teachers' Association, which he assisted to organize in 1854. From 1862 to 1871 he was editor of the Indiana School Journal.

Hon. Barnabas C. Hobbs, LL. D., was born in Washington County, Ind., 1815, and hence was familiar with pioneer life.

He received instruction, first in the "Old log school-house," and afterwards in the County Seminary presided over by John I. Morrison.

Later, he attended Cincinnati College, where he received instructions from Dr. W. H. McGuffey, Prof. O. M. Mitchel, and Hon. Edward D. Mansfield. He taught four years in Jefferson County, Ohio, as principal of Mt. Pleasant Boarding School.

In 1843, he came to Richmond, Ind., where he remained, teaching some years, part of the time in the Friends' Boarding School, since, Earlham College. In

1851, he went to Parke County, and took charge of the Bloomingdale Academy, where he remained fifteen years. He was an early member of the Indiana State Teachers' Association, and a strong advocate of Normal Schools. After serving two years as first president of Earlham College, he was elected to the office of Superintendent of Public Instruction. He advocated and succeeded in securing the establishment by the state of a reform school for juvenile offenders. The degree of A. M. was conferred upon him by Wabash College in 1858, and that of LL. D. by the State University in 1870. In 1871, he returned to Bloomingdale, where he still resides. He is a member of the Normal School Board, and of the Board of Trustees of the Terre Haute Polytechnic Institute.

HON. MILTON B. HOPKINS was born April, 1821, in Nicholas County, Ky. His early advantages for an education were not good, but his industry was untiring, his ambition great. With these, by the aid of a private tutor, he mastered Latin and Greek. In 1842, he married and commenced preaching at Milroy, Rush County, Ind. We next find him in Cincinnati as one of the editors of the American Christian Review. His health giving way, he returned to Rush County.

He was then, successively, teacher of district school in Rush County; Principal of Farmer's Academy, Clinton County; Principal of the High School in Boone County; Principal of Ladoga Academy, Montgomery County; and president of Howard College of Howard County. In 1870, he was elected Superintendent of Public Instruction, and in 1872, was re-elected to the same office. Aug. 16, 1874, he died at his residence in Kokomo. His manly common sense and logical frame of mind compensated in a measure for his lack of early training. In his talks with trustees and county officers, he was eminently successful in enlisting them in the work of education. In this popular work, his office never had a superior in this State. He was a man of great sociability, courtesy, and politeness. In his death the State lost an eminent and faithful citizen, and his family a good husband and father.

Hon. A. C. Hopkins, son of the above, filled very satisfactorily the unexpired term caused by the death of the father.

Hon. James H. Smart was born in June, 1841, in Centre Harbor, N. H. He received his early education in the school of his father, Dr. W. H. Smart, who was one of the old New England school-masters. He obtained a thorough academic education, with special reference to being fitted for the teacher's profession. He commenced teaching in 1858, and will thus, at the close of his present term of office, have been in the profession more than eighteen years. He was associate editor of the New Hampshire Journal of Education, and taught in various village schools in New Hampshire for four years. In 1863, he removed to Toledo, Ohio, where he remained for two and a half years, teaching in responsible positions; he was then elected superintendent of the public schools of the city of Fort Wayne. This position he held for ten years, during which time his schools bore a reputation for discipline, scholarship, and general advancement, second to none in the State. He was a member of the State Board of Education, also, in 1873, was President of the State Teacher's Association. In 1874, he was elected State Superintendent of the public schools of Indiana. In the same year, Dartmouth College conferred on him the honorary degree of Master of Arts. His untiring energy and powers of organization have brought him great credit as State Superintendent.

MEMBERS OF STATE BOARD OF EDUCATION.

GEORGE P. BROWN was born November 10th, 1836, in Ashtabula County, Ohio, and received his school education at Grand River Institute in Austinburgh, Ohio. He taught his first school in the winter of 1852–3. In 1854, he taught in Geauga County. From 1855 to 1860, he was principal of a union school in Waynesville, Ohio. From 1860 to 1865 he was superintendent of schools in Richmond, Ind. During the school year of 1865–6, he superintended the schools of New Albany. The next two years he was again in Richmond. He took charge of the Indianapolis High School in February, 1871, and was elected superintendent of the Indianapolis public schools, in place of A. C. Shortridge, resigned, in June, 1874. He is Secretary of the State Board of Education, has been connected with several educational periodicals, and is now associate editor of the Indiana School Journal. The different positions held by him, indicate the merit of the man. He has proven himself to be one of the ablest educators of the West.

JOHN M. BLOSS was born January 21, 1839, in Washington County, Ind. His early education was obtained in the common schools. In 1854, at the age of fifteen, he entered Hanover College, from which he graduated in 1860, receiving the degree of A. B. In 1858–9, he was Tutor, and in 1860–1, he had charge of the schools of Livonia. At this time he volunteered in the 27th Indiana Infantry, with which he remained until the close of the year 1864, when he entered the Ohio Medical College and took one course of lectures. In 1865–6, he taught at New Philadelphia. The four years next ensuing he was principal of the Orleans Academy. From 1870 to 1875, he had charge of the Female High School in New Albany, during which time eighty-six pupils graduated, many of whom are now teaching. In 1875, he was elected to the superintendency of the Evansville public schools, which position he now holds. Since 1867, Prof. Bloss has done much valuable work in institutes in the southern part of the State. Prof. Bloss holds the second position as city superintendent in the State. Being young, modest, and a good student, his life gives promise of much usefulness.

JOHN S. IRWIN was born April 4, 1825; took the degree of A.B. at the Western University of Pennsylvania in August, 1842, and the degree of M. D. at the University of Pennsylvania in 1847. He was married at Pittsburgh, September 30, 1847, to Miss Martha C. Mahon. On account of ill health he was forced to abandon his profession, and took a position in the banking house of Allen Hamilton & Co., at Fort Wayne, Indiana, Dec. 8, 1853. In 1865, he was appointed a member of the Board of Education for the city of Fort Wayne, and became Treasurer thereof, holding both positions until 1875. In 1870, he was made a member of the Board of Trustees for the State University, holding the position till January, 1876, when he resigned on account of becoming a member of the State Board of Education. In June, 1875, he was elected Superintendent of the Public Schools of the city of Fort Wayne, *vice* Prof. Smart, now State Superintendent. In July, 1875, the State University conferred upon him the honorary degree of LL.D. Dr. Irwin's cultivated literary tastes have led him much among old books, of which he has a large and well selected library. He is a genial Christian gentleman.

The other members of the State Board of Education are: Governor Thos. A. Hendricks, J. H. Smart, Dr. Lemuel Moss, Wm. A. Jones, and Hon. E. E. White, president-elect of Purdue University.

OTHER PROMINENT TEACHERS AND SUPERINTENDENTS.

A. J. VAWTER was born September 12, 1823, in Jefferson County, Indiana. His early education was neglected. At the age of twenty-one, feeling the need of better culture, almost without money, he left the home of his boyhood and went among strangers to seek an education. For five years he studied in what is now Franklin College, paying his way by manual labor, after which he was one of its teachers for one year. He next taught in the county seminary, at Shelbyville, Ind., for four years. He was one of the original signers of the call which resulted in the formation of the State Teachers' Association, of which he was a member for many years. In 1855, he became superintendent of the public schools of Lafayette, which position he held at the time the graded-schools were prostrated by the adverse decision of the Supreme Court. After this he struggled on to bring the public sentiment of the State to a higher standard until 1862, when he retired from the public school work. He was one of the early advocates of a State Educational Journal, a State Normal School, and County Superintendency, all of which he has lived to see established. More recently he has been connected with Ladoga Seminary. Thousands of young people have received their education in whole or in part under his direction, many of whom are to-day honored members of the various professions.

THOMAS CHARLES is a native of Wayne County, Indiana, and was brought up on a farm, attending winter schools irregularly between corn-gathering and sugar-making. In 1851, he commenced teaching in the schools of Randolph and Wayne counties. He remained until 1854, when he entered Antioch College, Ohio, under the presidency of Horace Mann. He graduated in 1860, and immediately after commenced teaching, expecting to make it his business for life. He first established the Economy High School, and then the Newport High School, both of which were attended by many boarding pupils from surrounding townships and counties. In 1866, he became principal of the Indianapolis City Academy, which he conducted for three years. In 1869, he removed to Chicago to act as agent for the New York house of Charles Scribner & Co., with which he is still connected.

*DANIEL HOUGH was born of Quaker parents, June 11, 1827, in New Garden, Wayne County, Indiana. He attended the Friends' school of his native place, summer and winter, from his sixth to his twelfth year. The next five years he worked on a farm in summer,

* Written by the Editor.

and attended school in winter, at Beech Grove Seminary in Union County, and in the home school. In his eighteenth year he commenced teaching in the village school at home. He graduated in Farmer's College, near Cincinnati, Ohio, in 1849, under the tuition of Dr. R. H. Bishop, formerly president of Miami University. After teaching a short time in Leesburg, Ohio, he went to Cincinnati and commenced as an assistant in the public schools in the spring of 1850. Two years later he was made principal, and he continued in this position till September, 1864, when he resigned and accepted a traveling agency for the house of Wilson, Hinkle & Co., of Cincinnati. Since 1866, he has been located in Indiana, and has done much valuable and gratuitous work as an instructor and lecturer in Teachers' Institutes. Upon leaving Cincinnati, the city superintendent, Mr. Harding, in his report speaks of Mr. Hough as follows: "For over fourteen years Mr. Hough gave his undivided attention to whatever would give efficiency to the school over which he presided. A more untiring, enthusiastic devotee to his profession it would be difficult to find. In attention to primary instruction, Mr. Hough stood in the front rank. No one better understood the wants of that department, and no one was more fertile in expedients to establish it on the right basis."

D. Eckley Hunter, son of Rev. Hiram A. Hunter, and grandson of Major David Robb, was born January 6, 1834, in Princeton, Indiana. He obtained his education as he could get it—first, in occasional country schools, and afterwards in seminaries and private schools at Princeton, Ind., Owensboro, Ky., and in the State University. He commenced teaching at the age of sixteen, in Gibson County, at sixteen dollars per month. He taught two years in the district schools of Knox County, and one year in Monroe; was two years principal of Bainbridge Academy in Putnam County, taught five years in Bloomington, was the founder of the graded-schools of that place, for three years was superintendent at Peru, and seven years at Princeton. He organized the graded-school at Princeton in 1860, and the high school in 1871. His institute work and educational lectures have extended to more than forty counties in Indiana. In 1869, he was elected President of the Indiana State Teachers' Association, of which he had been a member since 1856. He was elected President of the Primary Section of that body in 1870, and to the same office in the Superintendent's Section in 1871. In 1875, he was elected for life to the office of Permanent Secretary and *ex-officio* Treasurer in the same organization. He is the author of "Primary Charts," "Historical Cards," and "Object Lessons in Arithmetic and Inventive Drawing."

WM. A. BELL was born January 30, 1833, in Clinton County, Indiana, where he resided until his twentieth year. His early education was such as the common schools of the county afforded. In 1853, he entered the preparatory department of Antioch College, under President Horace Mann. After seven years he graduated in 1860, and in the fall of that year went to Mississippi to teach, but the war compelled him to return. In 1861, he took charge of the schools of Williamsburg, Wayne County, where he remained two years. He was elected principal of the Second Ward School in Indianapolis in 1863, and the next year was made principal of the high school. In

1865, he was superintendent of the schools of Richmond, Ind., but the next year again returned to the principalship of the Indianapolis High School, which place he continued to fill until 1871. July 20, 1871, he was married to Miss Eliza C. Cannell. He served as School Examiner of Marion County for four years, when the office of County Superintendent was created. In August, 1871, he became sole proprietor of the *Indiana School Journal*, and since that date has devoted his time to its interests, increasing its circulation to 4,000. In 1873, he was President of the State Teachers' Association. The last four years he has traveled much over the State, and has done excellent service in teacher's institutes. He is now a member of the Indianapolis school board. He is much loved and respected by all who know the value of a good man.

JOHN M. OLCOTT was born in 1833, in Dearborn County, Indiana. His father was from Waterbury, Conn., and his mother from Poughkeepsie, N. Y. His elementary education was obtained at home, his father having been a teacher. In 1850, at seventeen, he taught his first school, and in the year following entered Indiana Asbury University, from which he graduated in 1856. Immediately after graduating he was appointed superintendent of the schools of Lawrenceburgh, the county-seat of his native county, which position he held for four years. He was next superintendent of the Columbus (Ind.) schools for three years, and in 1863, he accepted the superintendency of the public schools of Terre Haute, in which position he labored for six years. Mr. Olcott was also County Examiner for Vigo County three years. In 1865, he was appointed a member of the Board of Trustees of the State Normal School, which place he held four years, acting as Secretary of the Board and Chairman of the Building Committee. In 1869, he was elected Professor of Mathematics in the State Normal School, which position he soon after resigned. Within the past decade he has done much institute work in the State. During the past five years he has been agent of Harper & Brothers, of N. Y.

ALEXANDER M. GOW descended from a Scotch-Irish ancestry, and was born in Washington, Washington County, Pennsylvania, 1828. He graduated at Washington College in 1847, and soon commenced the study of law. This work was suspended for a time while he took charge for seven years of the schools of his native town. In 1857 he was admitted to the bar, but the same year he removed to Dixon, Ill., and again engaged in teaching. After a residence of ten years in that State, filling the positions of Superintendent of Dixon public schools and of Rock Island city schools, member of the State Board of Examiners, and editor of the *Illinois Teacher*, he came to Indiana as Superintendent of the Evansville public schools. The work done by Mr. Gow in these schools during the eight years he had charge of them has not been surpassed in any other city in the State. As a member of the State Board of Education, he has been identified with some of the prominent educational reforms of the State. In 1870, he was elected president of the Indiana State Teachers' Association. He is the author of a widely circulated work, entitled "Good Morals and Gentle Manners." He still resides at Evansville, Ind., and is prominently connected with the Educational Department of the Centennial movement.

WM. H. WILEY was born in Rush County, Indiana, December 28, 1842. In September 23, 1859, he entered the preparatory school of the North-western Christian University, where he graduated from the classical department, June 24, 1864. After graduating from Bryant and Spencer's Commercial School, the degree of A.M. was conferred upon him by his *alma mater*, the North-western Christian University. April 1, 1865, he commenced his work in Terre Haute as principal of the Fourth District School. The same year he was elected principal of the Terre Haute high school. This position he held four years, when he was elected superintendent, a position he has now held seven years. Mr. Wiley has attended the meetings of the State Teachers' Association since 1865. This body elected him president at its last meeting, December, 1875. Mr. Wiley is a good example of patient, persevering industry, united with a kind and gentle disposition. He has deserved success.

J. T. MERRILL was born April 11, 1839, near Granville, Ohio. His parents died in his early youth, since which time he has worked his own way, managing to earn enough each summer to pay his way through school in the winter. In 1856, having saved $100, he entered Otterbein University, from which he graduated in 1862, being a tutor in the preparatory department while finishing his junior and senior years. He taught two years in Ohio; then removed to Lafayette, and became principal of the high school. In 1865, he married Miss Gertrude Deming, daughter of Dr. Elizur Deming. In 1867, he was elected superintendent of the Lafayette schools, which position he now holds.

SHERIDAN COX, of Kokomo, was born in Harrison County, Ohio, Dec. 20, 1833; in 1834, was taken by his parents to Coshocton County, where he worked on the farm during the summer and attended the district schools in the winter; commenced teaching in 1854; taught district schools four winters, attending preparatory schools during the summers, two of which were spent at the McNeely Normal School of Ohio; entered the Ohio Wesleyan University in 1858, from which he was graduated in 1862; distinguished while in college for proficiency in mathematics; receiving the degree of A. M. in 1865; removed to Illinois in 1862, where he taught Latin and Greek one year in Marshall College; in 1863, returned to Ohio and superintended the Roscoe Graded-Schools; in 1864, superintended the Canal Dover Union School; removed to Indiana in 1865, and taught the Winchester Seminary one year; was principal of the Logansport High School in 1866; in 1867, was made superintendent of all the Logansport public schools which he organized and graded; remained there seven years, during which period the number of teachers increased from eleven to twenty-three, and the number of pupils from five hundred to sixteen hundred; in 1873, took charge of the Kokomo public schools where he is still meeting with eminent success.

HAMILTON S. MCRAE was born in Harrison County, Ind. He was educated at the State University at Bloomington, where he graduated in 1857. After teaching one year in Maple Grove Academy, in Knox County, Ind., he commenced the study of law, which he practiced at Salem until the breaking out of the war. In 1861, he enlisted, and served until wounded and discharged. He has since been identified with the public school interests of the State, first, as principal of a ward building in Terre Haute, and afterwards as superintendent of schools at Vevay. During the past nine years, he has been doing good service as superintendent of the schools at Muncie.

MRS. EMMA (MONTGOMERY) MCRAE, wife of the above, and daughter of Rev. ——— Montgomery, of the M. E. Church, has been a successful teacher for more than ten years, and has greatly assisted her husband in the valuable work that has been done at Muncie. Both have done good service in the Indiana State Teachers' Association, and in numerous county and State institutes.

REV. J. H. MARTIN was born October 11, 1833, in Fayette County, Pa. He was educated at Woodvale Academy, Pa., and at the Ohio Wesleyan University. He taught from 1856 to 1859 in Middletown, Pa., when he came to Indiana, and was soon after made superintendent of the graded-schools at Franklin. In 1864, he became superintendent of the schools of Edinburgh and in 1866, he accepted the presidency of Brookvillle College. This position he resigned in 1869, because of the ill-health of his wife, and returned to Edinburgh to superintend the schools. In 1870, he was elected president of Moore's Hill College. Here he remained two years. In 1875, he was elected superintendent of the schools of Franklin and of the county of Johnson, both of which positions he now holds.

Prof. Martin is an earnest man, and is ardently attached to his profession. This, with his ability, and the assistance of a noble wife make him eminently successful, whether in the pulpit or in the school-room.

JOHN COOPER was born in Augusta County, Va.,

1827. The family removed first to Ohio, and afterward to Randolph County, Ind. In 1843, Mr. Cooper entered the county seminary at Winchester, Ind., under the superintendency of Rev. James S. Ferris. Here he remained three years, and then spent a number of years in teaching, continuing his studies in the meantime, and graduating at Miami University in 1857. Mr. Cooper's school-work has been one year in the district schools, four years as principal at Bluffton, thirteen years at Dublin, two years at New Castle, four years at Winchester, and two years as superintendent of the Richmond schools. He has also been a member of the Indiana State Teachers' Association from its organization in 1854, and for many years has been regarded as one of the leading educators of the State.

OLIVER H. SMITH was born June 2, 1831, in Fayette County, Ind. When he was six years old his father died, leaving his mother in limited circumstances. His early education, was, therefore, somewhat neglected. In 1850, after having had his muscles hardened by an apprenticeship of four years at a trade, he entered Indiana Asbury University, from which he graduated in 1856, and received the degree of A. M. in 1859. He was next principal of Thorntown Academy for six years, then of Danville Academy for two years. In 1862, he was elected president of Rockport Collegiate Institute, which position he held for four years. The next three years he was minister of the M. E. Church at Bloomington and at Bedford. In 1873, he was elected superintendent of the Jeffersonville public schools, which position he held two years. Then he was elected to superintend the public schools of Rockport, which position he now holds.

John K. Waltz was born February 24, 1840, in Floyd County, Indiana. His early education was obtained in district schools at home, and in Hedding Seminary, Ill. In 1862, he entered Indiana Asbury University, from which he graduated in 1867, receiving the degree of A. M. in 1870. He commenced teaching in 1860 in Floyd County; in 1867, he taught at Moore's Hill College; in 1868, he was superintendent at Attica; in 1869, principal in Indianapolis; in 1870, superintendent at Elkhart; and in 1874, superintendent at Logansport, which position he now fills.

W. A. Boles was born July 7, 1831, in Saratoga County, New York. He received a common school education in Trumbull County, Ohio. He served an apprenticeship and learned the trade of harness making; worked at his trade nights and mornings, and attended school. He taught his first school in Summit County, Ohio, at $13 per month and "boarded round." He commenced teaching in 1851 in central Kentucky, and afterwards taught in the following places: New Albany, Ind., Louisville, Ky., five years, and as superintendent of the Shelbyville, Ind., schools since 1868. Mr. Boles has the ability to keep up the interest in his schools.

David Graham was born January 13, 1826, in Franklin County, Ohio. He was educated in the common schools, in Reynoldsburg Academy, Ohio, and in Hanover College, Ind. He taught in the common schools of Ohio from 1846 to 1853. In 1853, he removed to Indiana and took a principal's place in the New Washington graded-schools, Clarke Co. In 1862, he taught in Madison, Ind. He superintended the Madison schools for two years. In 1865, he was elected superintendent of the Columbus, Ind., schools, which position he held four years, when he was elected to superintend the Rushville graded-schools, which position he holds at the present time. He is a faithful and successful superintendent, and an upright Christian gentleman.

D. D. BLAKEMAN was born November 30, 1832, in Otsego County, New York. He was educated at Michigan Central College, now Hillsdale College. He commenced teaching in 1852 in Michigan, and in 1854 removed to Kentucky, where he taught eight years. In 1862, he moved to Franklin County, Indiana, where he taught nine years, the last year in Brookville College. In 1871, he was made superintendent of the schools of Delphi, which position he now holds.

ROBERT NEWMAN JOHN, son of Dr. Jehu John, was born February 21, 1835, in Louisiana. His early education was obtained in the common schools of Ohio. He entered Miami University in 1855, and in 1858 he graduated, receiving the degree of B.A. Commencing in 1853, he taught in the public schools of Ohio for two years; in 1858, was principal of the high school in Harrison, Ohio; from 1860 to 1870, he taught in Franklin County, Ind., most of the time as principal of the Fairfield Academy; in 1870, was Professor of Mathematics in West Brook Seminary, Maine; in 1873, at Fairfield, Ind., again as minister; and in 1875, was made president of Smithson College at Logansport, which position he still holds.

J. G. ADAMS was born April 5, 1844, in Washington County, Pennsylvania. He attended Dunlap's Creek Academy to prepare for college. In 1866 he graduated at Iron City Commercial College. The next two years were spent in teaching to obtain money to complete his college course, which he did at Waynesburg College, Pa., in 1870. On leaving college, he taught in Beverly Academy, Ohio, and in Bethlehem Academy, Kentucky, in 1871. In 1873, he received the degree of A.M. from his *alma mater*, and was made principal of Beverly Academy, Ohio. In 1875, he was elected superintendent of the public schools of Rensselaer, in Jasper County, Ind., which position he now holds, and in which the leading paper of the place says he is winning golden opinions from both parents and pupils.

B. F. NIESZ was born November 16, 1842, in Canton, Ohio. His early life was spent on a farm, receiving a country district school education. At eighteen years of age he entered Mt. Union College, from which he graduated. In the autumn of 1871, he was one of three that organized the Northwestern Normal School, at Ada, Ohio. In 1873, he was appointed superintendent of the schools of Kentland, Ind. He was also appointed superintendent of the county, which position he now holds.

WM. H. CHURCHMAN, founder and present superintendent of the Indiana Institute for the Education of the Blind, was born November 29, 1818, near Baltimore, Md. At the age of seventeen, while attending school in New York City, he lost his sight. He then entered the Pennsylvania Institution for the Blind, at Philadelphia, from which he graduated in November, 1839. From the spring of 1840 to the summer of 1843, he was employed in the Ohio Institution for the Blind. In November, 1843, he removed to Nashville, Tenn., where, in the following spring, he organized the

Tennessee Institute for the Blind. He resigned in July, 1846, and removed to Indiana, where, in 1847, he founded and assumed the charge of the Indiana Blind Asylum.

In October, 1853, he left the Indiana Institute, and in the following year founded the La Porte (Ind.) Female Institute, which he conducted as a private enterprise until the summer of 1856; when, his buildings having been destroyed by fire, he accepted the superintendency of the Wisconsin Institute for the Blind, which position he held for the five years next ensuing. In September, 1861, he resumed the charge of the Indiana Institution, which he has since retained in fact, though during a portion of the time, from September, 1866 to April, 1868, he was employed in organizing, as superintendent-elect, the New York State Institution for the Blind, at Batavia. Mr. Churchman is eminently fitted for the position he holds.

Instructors of the Deaf and Dumb School, for the State of Indiana, are as follows, viz: William Willard, a deaf mute, who was employed in 1844, was the first instructor. He acted as principal until July, 1845, and was succeeded by J. S. Brown, who served as principal until July 7, 1853, when he was succeeded by Thomas MacIntire, the present superintendent, who has faithfully and honorably filled the position for the past 23 years.

Dr. M. M. Wishard, *Superintendent of the Soldiers' Orphans' Home*, was born in Johnson County, Ind., where he resided during his earlier life. In the year 1857 he removed to Danville, Hendricks County, where he studied medicine. He enlisted as a private soldier in Company A, 53d Regiment Indiana Volunteers, January 1, 1862, and was appointed Hospital Steward in 1863; was afterwards mustered out for promotion, and appointed Acting Assistant Surgeon U. S. A. In 1864, he was appointed in charge of the general hospital at Indianapolis; and at the close of the war took charge of the hospital for disabled soldiers. In the spring of 1865, he was made superintendent of Indiana Soldiers' Orphans' Home, located at Knightstown, Ind., where he still remains, laboring faithfully and earnestly for the welfare of those under his charge.

REV. R. F. BREWINGTON is a native of Dearborn County, Ind. He graduated in the scientific course at Moore's Hill College in 1860; enlisted in the army, August, 1862, and was commissioned 1st Lieutenant of Company K, 168th Regiment Indiana Volunteers. He has spent thirteen years in teaching; four years in Moore's Hill College, two years as superintendent of the Greensburg graded-schools, and four years as superintendent of the Vevay graded-schools. He became a member of the Southeastern Indiana Conference of the M. E. Church in 1872. In June, 1873, he was appointed Chaplain of the Soldiers' Orphans' Home, at Knightstown, Ind. He also has general management of the schools at the Home.

Time and space fail me to speak of the following well known and worthy teachers:

Clarkson Davis, Spiceland; C. W. Harvey, Greensburg; James R. Hall, Cambridge City; H. B. Jacobs, New Albany; D. D. Luke, Goshen; A. J. Snoke, Princeton; L. R. Williams, Angola; J. A. Zeller, Evansville; H. B. Brown, Valparaiso; G. W. Hufford, New Castle; Lee Ault, Winchester; E. S. Miller,

Michigan City; E. H. Butler, Attica; John Binford, Greenfield; J. P. Funk, Corydon; R. A. Chase, Plymouth; G. W. Lee, Greencastle; J. C. Macpherson, Richmond; L. B. Swift, La Porte; J. M. Wallace, Columbus; A. J. Douglass, Columbia City; I. N. Payne, Jeffersonville; William Jay, Earlham College; M. A. Barnet, Elkhart; J. W. Caldwell, Seymour; J. R. Trisler, Lawrenceburgh; A. J. Charlton, Vincennes; D. Mowry, Goshen; P. P. Stultz, Rising Sun; Timothy Wilson, Spiceland; William Pinkham, Paoli; W. H. Valentine, Terre Haute; A. H. Graham, Columbus; J. L. Rippitoe, Connersville, with a host of others who will be spoken of with reverence and affection as the school-masters of "ye olden time" by the biographer of the second centennial in 1976.

TEACHERS' ASSOCIATIONS, NORMAL SCHOOLS, LIBRARIES, ETC.

BY

GEORGE W. HOSS, LL.D.

ASSOCIATIONS, NORMAL SCHOOLS, LIBRARIES, ETC.

COUNTY ASSOCIATIONS.—The first county association of which I have knowledge was held in Wayne County, in 1838. The call for this meeting was issued by Jas. M. Poe and Ebenezer Bishop, teachers in Richmond. At a meeting held in 1841, there was a large attendance, and much interest was manifested. Henry Ward Beecher, then of Indianapolis, and Hon. E. D. Mansfield, of Ohio, were announced for addresses. The best information at hand indicates that after some years these associations ceased, and were revived, or a new organization formed in 1854. This latter continued until superseded by the institute.

The association here and throughout the State usually pioneered the institute, sometimes originating the same, and for the first few sessions, providing for its work, and supervising it. The association differed from the institute in being more discursive; the institute was more professional; hence the latter was a natural outgrowth of the former. Associations probably exerted their largest influence in the State from 1858 to 1863, and ceased, save in backward counties, by 1868. Probably every county in the State has had its association at some time in its educational history. No county, I presume, sustains one now. It has yielded to the institute, which is better adapted to present wants.

State Associations.—A State Educational Convention was held in Indianapolis in December, 1836. The attendance was large and the interest encouraging. Governor Noah Noble presided. Addresses were made by Prof. Jas. G. May, now of Salem, and by Dr. Andrew Wylie, then President of the State University. I find no records of any other meeting.

The Indiana State Teachers' Association.—In the summer of 1854 resolutions were passed at county associations, recommending the organization of a State association. In the autumn of that year a circular, signed by several of the leading educators of the State was issued, calling a meeting of the teachers and friends of education for the purpose of organizing a State Association. In pursuance of this call, the meeting convened at Indianapolis, on the 25th of December, 1854. Dr. Wm. M. Daily, then President of the State University, was elected President, and Prof. Geo. A. Chase, Secretary. A constitution, prepared by Prof. Caleb Mills and others was presented, and the association was quickly organized and ready for business. At this session several leading educational topics were discussed, and other work was outlined for the future. Addresses were delivered by Horace Mann, Hon. E. D. Mansfield, Dr. Breckinridge, of Kentucky, and others. The session was one of interest, spirit, and harmony. The enrollment was 178, representing 33 counties.

This was the dawn of a new era in education in Indiana. Teachers were aroused and energized; there were evidences of common purposes and common agencies. Plans began to enlarge and unify; from this time there began to be system. All the advanced movements of the State were here discussed and encouraged, and in many cases directed by the association, not a few originating with it. Institutes, the Normal School, the Journal, Reform School, Colored Schools, superintendency in county, city, and State, taxation, school architecture and the like, including almost all possible phases of professional work, all here received attention, some their chief impulse. Up to 1859 the sessions were biennial, after that, annual. The attendance has ranged from 40 to 482 members. The smaller attendance occurred under the derangement of the school system, consequent upon an adverse decision of the Supreme Court—a decision that left a blight on the schools for more than a dozen years.

The following are the names of the various Presidents of the association, with dates of their election.

Wm. M. Daily,	elected,	1851.	Geo. W. Hoss,	elected,	1865.
Charles Barnes,	"	1855.	Jos. F. Tuttle,	"	1866.
James G. May,	"	1856.	A. C. Shortridge,	"	1867.
B. C. Hobbs,	"	1857.	Joseph Tingley,	"	1868.
Caleb Mills,	"	1858.	D. E. Hunter,	"	1869.
E. P. Cole,	"	1859.	Alex. M. Gow,	"	1870.
Geo. A. Irvin,	"	1860.	Wm. A. Bell,	"	1871.
Cyrus Nutt,	"	1861.	Jas. H. Smart,	"	1872.
A. R. Benton,	"	1862.	Wm. A. Jones,	"	1873.
B. F. Hoyt,	"	1863.	Geo. P. Brown,	"	1874.
R. T. Brown,	"	1864.	Wm. H. Wiley,	"	1875.

COLLEGIATE ASSOCIATION.—A call was issued in December, 1867, by the Superintendent of Public Instruction, Geo. W. Hoss, to the various colleges in the State. This circular asked the college faculties to meet for the purpose of organizing a permanent Collegiate Association. The meeting was held at New Albany in conjunction with the Teachers' Association, in the latter part of December, 1867. The organization was effected, and Dr. Cyrus Nutt, of the State University, was elected president. The association held annual meetings from that time until December, 1874, but it never accomplished the work contemplated in its organization, for the reason that college faculties never engaged with any heartiness in its plans. Consequent upon this lack of interest, it was in December, 1874, merged in the general association.

TEACHERS' INSTITUTES.—The institute is an outgrowth of the association. The institute is professional and technical; the association discursive and legislative. The first institute in the State, so far as I can learn, was held in Ontario, Lagrange County, in 1846. This was superintended by Professor Rufus Patch. Thirty members attended. The next year a session was held with a larger attendance. This was the seed-corn of institutes in Indiana, and Mr. Patch brought it from the East.

The Northern Indiana Teachers' Institute held its first session at Mishawaka, St. Joseph County, in October 1849; the attendance being about one hundred and twenty-five teachers. One session of this institute was held in La Porte, in the spring of 1850, and another in the same place in the fall of the same year. In April, 1851, a session was held at Mishawaka, at which a permanent organization was effected and officers elected; C. J. Conn, of Elkhart, being chosen president. In the fall of 1851, sessions were held at Elkhart, Warsaw, and Logansport, conducted by Prof. A. D. Wright, of Perrysburgh, Ohio. In December, 1853, at the session at South Bend, composed of teachers from Indiana and Michigan, the name of the organization was changed to "Northern Indiana and Southern Michigan Teachers' Institute." Rufus Patch was elected president of the new organization. This association issued reports for the purpose of disseminating its views and aiding the work. The report of 1852 contained forty-eight pages, and gave much valuable information. From this report we learn that from the time of organization to October, 1852, sixteen sessions, of two weeks each, had been held, with an aggregate attendance of over five hundred. This was labor with results. I have not the date at which this organization ceased. In 1854, Wayne County held her first institute under the supervision of Mr. Sweet, of New York. In 1855, a six weeks institute was held in Sullivan County, under the supervision of Judge Hargrave and Prof. A. P. Allen. In October, 1858, D. E. Hunter, A. J. Vawter, R. M. Johnson, and L. S. Kilburn, organized an itinerating institute to be held at various points on the railroad from Greencastle to Crawfordsville. During the two years of the existence of this organization, sessions were held at all or nearly all towns between the two points named. In 1860, the State Association appointed an institute committee for each congressional district, with instructions to hold, or cause to be held, so far as practicable, an institute in each county in the district, and report the result at the next session of the association. A like committee was appointed in 1861–2–3 and–4. The work accomplished by this agency was valuable, not only in work done, but in the spirit awakened, which bore fruit in subsequent years. This work was all voluntary on the part of teachers, there being no law requiring it nor money to aid it. In 1865, a law was passed requiring the County Examiner to hold in his county at least one institute each year, also making a small appropriation from the count, treasury in aid of the same. This aid was and now is $35 per annum when twenty teachers, or persons preparing to become such, attend, and $50 when forty at tend. This was the opening of the Institute period in Indiana. The first year after this enactment, fifty-eigh counties held institutes, with an aggregate attendance of 3,533. From all parts of the State word came to the office of Public Instruction announcing increased efficiency, and a quickened educational sentiment, consequent upon these institutes. They not only instructed but aroused. Concerning this efficiency, the Superintendent of Public Instruction, in his report to the legislature in 1867, said: "To say that the institutes are producing large and good results, is hardly an adequate statement of the facts; they are producing both larger and better results, in proportion to cost, than any other agency in our system." They are still yielding large and valuable results, although slight modifications might improve them.

TOWNSHIP INSTITUTES.—Township institutes, like the county gatherings, were at first volunteer efforts. The first of these, so far as I have information, was held in 1866. Hamilton S. McRae, then examiner of Switzerland County, held a Township Institute in said county in December, 1866. Near the same time, possibly the summer following, Wm. A. Bell held a similar institute in Marion County. Thus these volunteer efforts grew in favor and strength until 1873, when the legislature required Township Institutes by law. The act says "that at least one Saturday in each month, during which the public schools may be in progress, shall be devoted to Township Institutes and Model Schools for the improvement of teachers." These are effective agents for good.

STATE INSTITUTES.—A State Institute was held at Knightstown, Henry County, opening July 11, 1865, and continuing three weeks. Prof. J. M. Olcott was superintendent. He had suggested the idea of such an institute the year previous. The aggregate enrollment was 131. In each of the years 1866, 1867, and 1868, four State institutes were held in the four quarters of the State. The attendance in 1866, was 500; in 1867, 597, and in 1868, 462. The State institutes were under the management of a State Central Committee appointed by the State Teachers' Association. In 1873, the State Board of Education held institutes similar to the above.

TOWNSHIP LIBRARIES.—In 1852, an act was passed by the legislature levying a tax for the purpose of establishing Township Libraries. In pursuance of this provision, Superintendent Larrabee distributed in 1854 to the several townships in the State 143,728 volumes, at a cost of $147,422. In 1856, Superintendent Mills distributed about 100,000 volumes, at a cost of $110,000. In 1866, Superintendent Hoss distributed 29,918 volumes at a cost of $40,754. In 1867, a fund of $50,000 was raised for the same purpose, but on the recommendation of the State Superintendent this amount was appropriated to the building fund of the

Normal School. Since that time but slight additions have been made. The number of volumes in these libraries in 1875 was 264,858. There were taken out for reading during the year 198,496 volumes. These libraries are under the management of the township trustee, and are open to all citizens in the township. In theory these gave promise of great good, but practically they have not met the promise.

City Libraries.—As yet, we have but few city libraries. Our school system is not old enough to produce so mature fruit, but it is hoped that it will in a few years. I name a few of the more prominent libraries.

Muncie, Delaware County, has made a beginning; it has 2,190 volumes. This library was opened June, 1875. Superintendent H. S. McRae deserves much credit for this beginning.

Evansville has 8,000 volumes, with a daily circulation of 175 volumes. This library is under the control of the school board.

Richmond and the township, jointly, have 10,000 volumes. This library was opened in 1864. Robert Morrison donated $5,000 for books, and a commodious building, well furnished, for library and reading rooms.

Indianapolis has a library of 18,000 volumes; opened April 1, 1873, with 12,000 volumes; average daily circulation for year ending April, 1875, 342 volumes; minimum 156, and maximum 791. This library is under the management of the school board. These institutions are a perpetual blessing to multitudes, both rich and poor. A reading community can never be grossly ignorant or vicious.

College Libraries.—The number of volumes in our college libraries is as follows:

Merom College, Merom	1,000 volumes.
Normal School, Terre Haute	1,500 "
Franklin College, Franklin	2,000 "
North-western Christian University, Irvington .	2,200 "
Earlham College, Richmond	4,000 "
Indiana University, Bloomington . . .	6,500 "
Hanover College, Hanover	7,100 "
Notre Dame College, Notre Dame . . .	10,000 "
Asbury University, Greencastle . . .	10,000 "
Wabash College, Crawfordsville . . .	17,250 "
Total No. vols. in college libraries,	61,550 volumes.

Normal Schools.—In the first report issued from the office of Public Instruction in 1852, we would naturally expect a plea for Normal Schools. On the contrary, we find the following: "Our Indiana law makes no special provision for these," (*i. e.*, Normal Schools) "Perhaps it is well, for I doubt whether such schools . . . would comport with our circumstances, or suit our government, or meet our wants." This, and the utter silence of the next four or five reports, doubtless had much to do with the protracted delay of a Normal School. In the eighth annual report of the superintendent, we find language of a different character: "I fear," says the Superintendent, "we shall never realize that completeness of qualifications of teachers we desire . . . until the State adopts and carries into effect some plan for Normal School instruction." Prior to this, the teachers all over the State were urging the necessity of Normal Schools, yet they seemed to accomplish but little. In the State Association, also, the establishment of a Normal School had been frequently and persistently urged. At almost every session, until legislative action was taken, the subject received attention in some form. In 1857 an able report was read, followed by warm and lengthy discussion, ultimating in a committee to memorialize the legislature. At a subsequent session a committee was appointed to issue a circular to the people, informing them of the need for and benefits of such a school, and urging their co-operation. The people and the legislature were slow learners, hence years wore away before action was taken. At length the auspicious moment seemed to have come in the educational revival of 1865, and a Normal School bill was introduced in the House in the winter of that year. It passed the House, but was not reached in the Senate, consequently it went over as unfinished business. At the called session following, it passed the Senate and became a law December 20, 1865. The voice sent up by educators throughout the State was *gloria!* A struggle of eleven continuous years had culminated in victory.

Hon. B. E. Rhoads, of Vermillion County, was specially efficient in securing the passage of the bill. The law provided that the institution should be located in that city which should make the largest donation, but not less than $50,000. Terre Haute donated $50,000 in money, and added a site worth $25,000. No other place offered donations; consequently the Board of Normal School Trustees, at its meeting May 15, 1866, declared the institution located at Terre Haute. Prof. J. M. Olcott, then Superintendent of Terre Haute public schools, was prominently efficient in securing the location at this place. Steps were at once taken for the erection of a building, the dimensions of which are: length, 190 feet; width, 114 feet; height of walls, 67 feet; of towers, 152 feet. The total cost has been over $200,000.

The school opened in charge of W. A. Jones as president, and a competent faculty, January 6, 1870. The number of students at its opening was 21, and the number enrolled during the last academic year was 270. Total enrollment since opening, 1160; number of graduates, male, 14; female, 35; total number of graduates, 49; number of faculty, 8; volumes in library, 1,500. An integral part of the school is a model department, divided into intermediate and primary schools.

Before the institution was established, doubts were entertained whether one school could make itself perceptibly felt throughout the State. These doubts have, in the short period of five years, been removed from the minds of all who are well informed. This school is becoming a power among the educational appliances of the State. It is, as yet, the only Normal School the State has. There have been others established by private enterprise. There is now a large school at Valparaiso, and there are also several training schools connected with high schools. The State University has had, at several times, what was called a "Normal Department." It organized such a class in 1854, but discontinued it in 1856. It re-opened the department in 1865 and maintained it one year. It started again in 1868, but the trustees, in 1870, finally decided to abandon the work, in view of the fact that the school at Terre Haute had opened with adequate facilities for all.

School Journals.—In October, 1846, Mr. H. F. West, of Indianapolis, started a small journal, entitled the *Common School Advocate*. He published one number only. This was the first educational publication known in the State.

In January, 1852, A. D. Wright, from Perrysburgh, Ohio, commenced the publication of a paper called the *Educationist*. It was issued from Indianapolis; the third number terminated the enterprise, so far as I can learn.

At the first session of the State Teachers' Association (1854), the subject of an Educational Journal was considered. After a comparison of views the project was referred to the Executive Committee, with instructions to report at the next session of the association. The report was made in due time and the following action was taken: "*Resolved*, 1. That this association will publish an Educational Journal, similar in size and typographical execution to the Ohio Journal of Education. 2. That this journal be conducted by nine editors appointed by the association, one of whom shall be styled Resident Editor." The corps of editors selected was Geo. B. Stone, Resident Editor; Associates, W. D. Henkle, E. P. Cole, Geo. A. Chase, Rufus Patch, B. F. Hoyt, Mary Wells, Jane Chamberlain. The paper was named the *Indiana School Journal*, and this name it has borne to the present time. Members of the association subscribed for five hundred copies, and the publishing house of W. B. Smith & Co., of Cincinnati, donated $200 to aid the enterprise. In January, 1856, was issued the first number. Professor E. P. Cole served as traveling agent for the journal for a few months, and as a result the subscription became large for a new publication, but it soon afterwards was somewhat diminished. In 1858, G. B. Stone left the

State and Prof. W. D. Henkle became the editor. Mr. Henkle left the State in August, 1859, and O. Phelps became editor. The association, at its session in December, 1859, transferred the management of the Journal, with some slight reservation, to Mr. Phelps. In 1862, Mr. Phelps transferred the Journal to Geo. W. Hoss. In consequence of Mr. Phelps' ill-health, as well as his absence from the State, the circulation of the Journal had become quite limited, not exceeding 150 paying subscribers; but in 1866, the circulation reached 1,100. In July, 1869, Wm. A. Bell became half owner of the Journal. In July, 1871, Prof. Hoss, having been elected president of the Kansas State Normal school, sold his remaining interest to Mr. Bell. The Journal has continued to increase in circulation and favor until its monthly issue is 4,000, among the largest (if not the largest) in the United States. In March, 1875, A. C. Shortridge and Geo. P. Brown became associate editors and publishers, but Mr. Shortridge has recently transferred his interest to W. A. Bell. From its first issue, this Journal has been a power in the educational work of the State; always progressive, sometimes aggressive; seconding all advances, sometimes happily and ably leading. Its future promises larger work and greater usefulness.

A youths' school paper, called the *Little Chief*, published by Prof. Shortridge at Indianapolis, made its first issue in January, 1867. It continued several years, reaching at one time a circulation of 1,200.

The *Indiana Teacher*, published at Indianapolis, made its first appearance in January, 1869, and in six months was consolidated with the School Journal.

The *Educationist*, published at Indianapolis by Prof.

A. C. Shortridge and Prof. Geo. P. Brown, was first issued in January, 1873, and continued until December, 1874, when it united with the Journal. The Journal, like Aaron's rod, has been swallowing the rest.

The *Northern Indiana Teacher*, edited by Prof. H. A. Ford, issued its first number from South Bend in January, 1874. In October, 1875, the circulation was 900. It is ably edited.

So great is the educational system in our State that it has been deemed wise to give it a tongue. These journals have given utterance to the educational thought of the State. It is hoped they will never speak less pointedly or forcefully than they now do.

COLLEGES AND COLLEGE WORK.

BY

WILLIAM A. BELL, A.M.

COLLEGES AND COLLEGE WORK.

THE history of the colleges of any commonwealth is always an interesting study, as their number and character are a sure index to the enterprise and intelligence of the people. It is a remarkable fact that educational institutions grow downward. Instead of the primary schools coming first, and the academies and colleges growing out of them, the reverse is true. In all countries, colleges have preceded lower schools. The ruling classes have always been the educated classes, and just in proportion as the common people have gained the franchise and the right to help rule, have they provided themselves with the facilities for obtaining an education. It is no more true that an army, to be under discipline and to be successful, must have well educated and well trained officers, than it is that society to be well regulated and prosperous must have well educated and cultured law-makers and leaders. To reduce generals, and colonels, and captains to the rank of the common soldier, both in education and position, would presage no more certainly the demoralization and utter overthrow of an army, than cutting off all higher education would foretell with certainty, not only a halt in the march of civilization, but a speedy return to barbarism. It is as essential to the welfare of a State that its leaders be thoroughly educated, as it is that its voters have a common school education. In an important sense, then, the colleges are the life of the State.

The brief histories given below have been prepared, for the most part, from sketches furnished by presidents or others connected with the various colleges. They are as full as the space allotted to this subject would allow. It is hoped that enough of the main facts have been given to enable the reader to gain a fair idea of the origin, growth, and present condition of the institutions named.

VINCENNES UNIVERSITY.—In 1804, Congress authorized one township of land to be reserved in each of the three land districts (Detroit, Vincennes, and Kaskaskia) of Indiana territory, for the establishment of seminaries of learning. The township for the Vincennes district, containing 23,040 acres, was located in Gibson County, Ind., October 10, 1806, by Albert Gallatin, Secretary of the Treasury. September 17, 1807, the territorial legislature chartered the University, locating it at Vincennes, and granted it the lands in Gibson County. December 6, 1807, the board of trustees organized with William Henry Harrison, John Gibson, Henry Vanderburgh, Francis Vigo, and twenty other distinguished citizens, as members. Gen. Harrison was made president of the board, and continued as such until 1811. About 4,000 acres of the land were sold by order of the legislature, and a large brick building was erected at Vincennes costing $6,000, which took most of the proceeds. A grammar school, to which was added the study of languages and mathematics, was opened, but as it was dependent almost entirely upon tuition fees for its support, it had a hard struggle for existence.

Rev. Samuel T. Scott was the first president. He filled the office until 1823, when Rev. Henry M. Shaw was made president. Soon after this, the University suspended for want of funds. In 1822 the remainder of the Gibson County land was sold by the State, and the proceeds applied to the State University at Bloomington.

In 1828 the county of Knox established the Knox County Seminary in the building belonging to the University. The old university board held no meeting from 1823 till 1838, when there was a reorganization, with Thomas Alexander as president. The old building and grounds were sold to the Catholic Church for a small sum. In 1840, with the very limited means at command, the trustees again re-opened the institution, and elected Rev. B. B. Killikelly, president.

In 1844, a large number of suits were commenced against the occupants of the university lands in Gibson County. Before these suits were decided, the legislature assumed the responsibility, and, in 1846, authorized the Vincennes University to commence action against the State in Marion Circuit Court. After much litigation in the local courts and in the Supreme Court of the United States, in 1854 a decision was obtained in favor of the University, and in 1855 the legislature authorized an issue of bonds to the amount of $66,585 in favor of the institution: $25,000 of this was retained by Samuel Judah, the attorney, agent, and secretary of the board, for services and expenses. The board brought suit against Mr. Judah for the amount, and obtained judgment in the Sullivan County Court, but on an appeal the judgment was reversed in the Supreme Court. This left the board with something more than $40,000, which gives an annual income of over $4,000.

Rev. R. M. Chapman was elected president of the University in 1855. He resigned in June, 1866. From 1866 to 1872, the school was at a low ebb. Ii 1872, Lewis Prugh, A. M., was elected president, with H. R. Gass and Miss Ray Piety as assistants, and since that time it has been in good condition. It is now a good classical school. The charter provides that "there shall be a Faculty not to exceed four professors," and that "the Latin, Greek, French, and English languages, together with mathematics, natural philosophy, logic, ancient and modern history, rhetoric, and the laws of nature and nations shall be taught." It also provides for departments of Law, Divinity, and Medicine, to be established at the pleasure of the board of trustees. "No particular tenet of religion shall be taught, and Indians shall be educated, maintained, and clothed free of expense. All students shall be educated gratis, as far as the funds will permit. Females shall be admitted, and a grammar school established, in which the rudimentary branches shall be taught." It also provides that "$20,000 shall be raised by a lottery, with which a library and philosophical apparatus shall be purchased." The terms of the charter have been but partially realized. The education of the Indians and the lottery scheme are still unfulfilled conditions.

The departments of Law, Divinity, and Medicine, have not been established, and can not be with the present income. Three years ago, Congress donated to the University all the vacant and unclaimed lands in Knox County, which will probably increase the endowment fund several thousand dollars. Students are required to pay a tuition fee of ten dollars a year. A small fund is annually accumulating which may be used to erect suitable buildings, of which the University stands greatly in need. The Vincennes University was the first school of a high order established in the territory north-west of the Ohio River.

THE INDIANA UNIVERSITY.—As early as the year 1804 Congress granted a township of land in Gibson County, and in 1816 another township in Monroe County for the support of a seminary of learning. By an act of the legislature in 1820, trustees of the seminary were appointed, and a meeting was held in Monroe County, at which the site for the seminary was selected. This has since become the Indiana University. It was not till 1825 that a building was ready for the opening of the school. The Rev. Baynard R. Hall took charge of the seminary at a salary of $150 per year. In 1827, Prof. John H. Harney was employed to teach mathematics and the physical sciences at a salary of $300 per year, the principal's salary having been raised to $400. In 1828, the legislature raised the seminary to the dignity of a college. The Rev. Andrew Wylie, D. D., was entrusted with the charge of the new institution. Dr. Wylie continued to preside until his death, in November, 1851. After an interval of nine months, during which time Prof. T. A. Wylie was acting-president, Alfred Ryors, D. D., was chosen to fill the vacancy. Dr. Ryors resigned in 1853, and was succeeded by Wm. M. Daily, D. D., who held the office till 1858. After an interval of nearly a year, Prof. T. A. Wylie again acting as president, John H. Lathrop, LL. D., was elected, but resigned in 1859. His successor was Cyrus Nutt, D.D., LL.D., who continued president till 1875. After his resignation, Lemuel Moss, D. D., was elected, and now holds the office.

At the time of the organization of the college, there was in Indiana but little demand for higher education. Wha was needed was fully supplied, and considering the resources of the institution, good work was done. In the year 1838, the college by an act of the legislature, was chartered as a University; its faculty was increased, and its field of work somewhat enlarged. In 1854, the college building was burned. All its contents, embracing a small, though valuable, library, together with the libraries of the literary societies, were destroyed. The philosophical and chemical apparatus, which were in another building, escaped destruction. About the same time, a suit which had been brought against the University by the trustees of Vincennes University was decided adversely to it, by which more than half its endowment fund was lost. Through the energy, however, of its trustees and of the faculty, the legislature was induced to make good the loss, and Congress also consented to grant another endowment, selected from congressional lands within the bounds of the State. A new and much more convenient building was completed in 1856, the citizens of Bloomington aiding very materially in the work. In a year or two the University was in a better condition than it had ever been before. In the year 1867, the legislature made an appropriation of $8,000, and in 1873, another appropriation of $15,000 was made, making in all $23,000; which, together with its former income, has put the University on a comparatively strong foundation. An additional building has recently been erected, for which appropriations were made by the legislature. In the new building there is a museum ninety-seven feet in length, by forty-seven in width, well lighted and fitted up for the display of a large collection of minerals and geological specimens of the late David Dale Owen, and for the reception of a complete set of Ward's casts. In the same building there is an analytical laboratory, provided with the appliances necessary to a thorough instruction in both quantitative and qualitative analysis. For the illustration of physical science, and for practical instruction in engineering and surveying, suitable apparatus and instruments are provided; all the departments, indeed, under the efficient management of the board, are furnished with such appliances as are necessary to the performance of good work. The library is not large, but it is well selected; it consists of about 6,000 volumes.

In the year 1840 a law school was organized, with one professor. Since the year 1844, this department has annually sent forth a graduated class. There are at present, two professors, who give instruction in this school during the three terms of the college year. The large and well furnished room and law library in the new college building, and the competent professors, afford excellent facilities for the study of law. Connected with the university, but located at Indianapolis, is a flourishing medical school. A preparatory department, in connection with the high school in Bloomington, has been established by the board, where candidates for the Freshman class may be thoroughly prepared, in common with others who may desire instruction in the same elementary branches.

The growth of the Indiana University, although not as rapid as that of some other institutions of the West, has at least been encouraging. The first Faculty, in 1828, consisted of a president and two professors, and a principal of the preparatory department. The present Faculty of Arts consists of a president, eight professors, and a principal of the preparatory department. The Faculty of Law consists of two professors. The Faculty of Medicine consists of nine, making twenty-one in all. The course of instruction in the university is extensive and thorough, and will compare favorably with that of any similar institution of equal means.

The present Faculty consists of Lemuel Moss, D. D., President and Professor of Moral, Mental, and Political Philosophy.

T. A. Wylie, D. D., LL. D., Professor of Natural Philosophy.

Richard Owen, M. D., LL. D., Professor of Natural Science.

Daniel Kirkwood, LL. D., Professor of Mathematics.

Rev. Elisha Ballantine, A. M., Professor of Greek Language and Literature.

Col. James Thompson, U. S. A., Professor of Civil Engineering.

Rev. Amzi Atwater, A. M., Professor of Latin Language and Literature.

George W. Hoss, LL. D., Professor of English Language, Literature, and Elocution.

Thomas C. Van Nuys, M. D., Professor of Chemistry.

Walter R. Houghton, A. M., Principal of Preparatory Department.

Hon. B. E. Rhoads, and Hon. Cyrus McNutt, Law professors.

HANOVER COLLEGE.—This was the third college established in Indiana. The initial steps were taken in 1825. They grew out of the necessity felt by the Presbyterian Church for a ministry raised at home; the East not being able to supply the demand. The Presbytery of Salem, then embracing Indiana and Illinois, appointed a committee to select a location and organize an academy. Hanover, Jefferson County, was selected as the location of the proposed school. The inhabitants of this town represented the best society of Kentucky, Virginia, Pennsylvania, and New Jersey, and were chiefly of Scotch-Irish descent. The place was healthful and the scenery unsurpassed. Its site on the Ohio river made it accessible to a large territory. It was then the center of Presbyterian influence in the State. Failing to secure a suitable principal, in 1826, the Presbytery requested the pastor, the Rev. John Finley Crowe, to open the academy. This he did on New Year's day, 1827, in a log cabin on his grounds. Here six boys opened their Latin grammars, and became the nucleus of Hanover College and the North-western Theological Seminary. A revival of religion in 1827, which brought into the church eight of its fourteen students, led to a large accession to the school.

Hanover Academy received its first charter December 30, 1828. A collegiate course was at once organized. In 1830, a Theological Department was established, and John Matthews of Virginia was called to its head. In 1833, the charter was amended, changing the title to Hanover College, and as such it opened under the presidency of James Blythe, D. D., of Kentucky, having the four college classes already organized and a preparatory department with a large number of students. Its first class graduated in 1834, and since that time it has sent forth graduates regularly each year. In the centennial year, the semi-centennial of the college, its list of Alumni will embrace over 425 names, of whom one-half are devoted to the ministry, over sixty are engaged in teaching, and the rest are distributed chiefly in the legal and medical professions. Of about four thousand matriculates, the most of them received all their higher education at Hanover.

In 1843 a new charter, with university powers, was granted. Under it, as yet, but two courses have been organized, a Classical and a Scientific course, the two being parallel. Thus the entire force of the faculty is spent, as it were, upon one course of study. The buildings consist of the main college, a spacious and well arranged structure, a boarding-house, and one residence. Arrangements are making to erect in the Centennial year, a president's house and two additional dormitories. The grounds embrace over 200 acres. There are three endowed chairs with $65,000, besides a general endowment fund. There are fine libraries, cabinet, herbarium and apparatus. The property with the endowment amounts to $500,000.

A full list of the Presidents of this institution is as follows, viz.:

1832–1836, Rev. James Blythe, D. D.

1838–1843, Rev. Erasmus D. McMaster, D. D., LL. D.

1846–1849, Rev. Sylvester Scovel, D. D.

1849–1854, Rev. Thomas E. Thomas, D. D.

1855–1857, Rev. Jonathan Edwards, D. D., LL. D.

1859–1866, Rev. James Hood, D. D.

1868–1870, Rev. George D. Archibald, D. D.

1870——, Rev. Geo. C. Heckman, D. D.

Vice-President 1832–57, Rev. John Finley Crowe, D. D.

The present Faculty consists of Geo. C. Heckman, D. D., President and Professor of Ethics and Biblical Instruction.

Rev. S. Harrison Thomson, Ph. D., LL. D., Astronomy.

Rev. Joshua B. Garritt, A. M., Greek Language and Literature.

Rev. Edward J. Hamilton, A. M., Logic and Mental Philosophy.

John M. Coulter, A. M., Natural Sciences, Latin Language and Literature.

Rev. W. Nevin Geddes, A. M., Mathematics and Mechanical Philosophy.

Frank Lyford Morse, A. M., Principal of Preparatory Department.

Hugh H. Young, A. M., Assistant Professor.

S. Wright Black and John H. Bright, Tutors.

WABASH COLLEGE.—This institution is situated at Crawfordsville. The town was laid out in the spring of 1822. In the fall of 1832, Judge Williamson Dunn offered fifteen acres of land at Crawfordsville as the site of a college, and this became the occasion of the remarkable meeting to which attention is called. November 21, 1832, a meeting was held at the house of the Rev. James Thompson, in Crawfordsville. The following persons were present. Rev. James Thompson, his brother Rev. John S. Thompson, Rev. James. A. Carraban, Rev. E. O. Hovey, Rev. John M. Ellis,

Elder John Gilliland, Hezekiah Robinson, and John McConnel. Mr. Ellis was from Illinois. On the 22d it was "unanimously resolved to be expedient to attempt the establishment of a literary institution at Crawfordsville in connection with manual labor."

On the evening of November 22, a public meeting was held to present the enterprise to the citizens of the town, and "a subscription was commenced towards the erection of a building on the site given by Williamson Dunn." The next morning five of the original convention visited the land which Dunn had given, and selected the spot upon which to erect the first building; and there, in solemn prayer, in the midst of Nature's unbroken stillness, they dedicated the enterprise to God, and invoked his blessing upon it. The ground was covered with snow, and the five men who thus bent the knee as in a consecrating act were, James and John S. Thompson, E. O. Hovey, James A. Carraban, and John M. Ellis. In December, 1833, the new building was in a condition to receive its first school, and on the third of that month Prof. Caleb Mills, a graduate of Dartmouth College and a classmate of Prof. Hovey, began the instruction in the college which has never been suspended. He commenced with twelve young men, and the sum pledged to the new college was $1,543.

The first name of the college was "The Wabash Manual Labor College and Teachers' Seminary." This was afterwards changed to its present name. In 1834, Elihu W. Baldwin was elected president. In 1835, the present site was purchased, and that summer the "Old Dormitory" was begun with funds procured, in part, in the East. It was not completed until 1838, when it was destroyed by fire, a calamity of whose dimensions we, in this day, can scarcely form an adequate idea.

Dr. Baldwin was inaugurated July 13, 1836. The first commencement occurred, July 11, 1838, and the building was burned, September 23, 1838. Dr. Baldwin lived to graduate the classes of '38, '39, and '40. He died October 15, 1840, universally regretted. In 1841, his successor, Charles White, D. D. was elected, and in July of the following year was inaugurated. He presided over the college twenty years, with distinguished ability and success. He died, October 29, 1861, having carried the institution through some dark and perilous periods. His successor, Joseph F. Tuttle, D. D., who is still president, began his labors in May, 1862, and was formally inaugurated on commencement day of that year.

The school, which in 1833 began with twelve students, has grown into an institution which has more than two hundred students. During that period it has educated, to some extent, several thousand young men. Its first class was graduated in 1838, and numbered two. The class of '76 numbers 24. Including the class of '76, the whole number of alumni is 318. Two of the original faculty, Prof. E. O. Hovey and Prof. Caleb Mills are still connected with the college. The faculty of instruction consists of twelve at the present time.

The institution has four buildings in a campus of thirty-three acres, the most of which is covered with a magnificent forest. The cabinets are rich and valuable, as is also the library, containing several thousand volumes, of which some 4,000 were placed on the shelves within the last year. Through the liberality of its friends, the college has an endowment which, with its other resources, makes it quite independent. In addition to the ordinary endowments, there is a large fund, the income of which is applied to aid certain classes of young men in their education.

The present Faculty consists of Joseph F. Tuttle, D. D., President, and Professor of Moral and Intellectual Philosophy.

Edmund O. Hovey, D. D., Professor of Chemistry and Geology.

Caleb Mills, A. M., Professor of the Greek Language and Literature.

Samuel S. Thomson, A. M., Professor of the Latin Language and Literature.

John L. Campbell, LL. D., Professor of Mathematics, Natural Philosophy, and Astronomy.

Wm. C. White, A. M., Professor of Rhetoric, and Teacher of the German and French Languages.

Col. Henry B. Carrington, LL. D., U. S. A., Professor of Military Science, by authority of the U. S. Government.

Daniel A. Bassett, A. M., Principal of the Preparatory Department.

Matthew M. Whiteford, A. M., Associate Principal of Preparatory Department.

Henry R. Thomson, A. M., Associate Professor of Chemistry.

Henry Z. McLain, A. M., Associate Professor of Greek.

Indiana Asbury University.—This University, situated at Greencastle, is under the patronage and control of the four conferences of the Methodist Episcopal

Church in Indiana. In the autumn of 1835, the Indiana Conference, which then embraced the whole State, determined to establish an institution of learning. The General Assembly considered that such an institution would be an advantage to the State, and passed an act January 27, 1837, establishing "The Indiana Asbury University, which shall be founded and maintained forever upon a plan the most suitable for the benefit of the youth of every class of citizens and of every religious denomination, who shall be freely admitted to equal advantages and privileges of education, and to all the literary honors of said university, according to their merit."

On the 5th of June, 1837, the preparatory department was opened by Cyrus Nutt, D. D., afterwards vice-president and professor of the University, and more recently president of the Indiana State University. In May, 1839, Matthew Simpson, D. D., now one of the bishops of the Methodist Episcopal Church, assumed the duties of his office as first president, and the various college departments were regularly organized. The first Commencement was held in 1840, in the chapel of the University, then just completed. Bishop Simpson was succeeded in 1849 by L. W. Berry, D. D. In 1854, Daniel Curry, D. D., was elected president. He was followed by Thomas Bowman, D. D. in 1858. On the resignation of Bishop Bowman, Reuben Andrus, D. D., was elected president, who, upon his retirement in 1875, was followed by Alexander Martin, D. D., the present incumbent.

In 1840, the faculty consisted of but three instructors. At present, there are ten professors and teachers fully employed in the work of instruction. In the first catalogue, published in 1839, the students numbered 85. The catalogue of 1875 shows an attendance of 451. The attendance this year exceeds that of any preceding year. At the beginning, the school was opened in a comparatively small and unpretending building. Now, in addition to the very substantial and capacious West Hall, the corner-stone of which was laid in June, 1837; the East Hall, a most imposing building, has been erected, and is this year occupied for the first time. The aggregate value of grounds, buildings, and collections, is estimated at $200,000. The productive endowment during the same time has risen to about $141,000. The growth of its cabinets, libraries, apparatus, etc., has been nearly in the same proportion. Among its most valuable appliances are the excellent literary societies, established and maintained by the students themselves. The entire number of those who have received the honors of the institution is 583. Besides the alumni, hundreds have received an academic education in the preparatory school of the University.

The control and management of the institution is mainly intrusted to a board of trustees, elected by the several annual conferences of the Methodist Episcopal Church in the State of Indiana. In the University proper there are at present three regular schools, or courses of study, viz.: the Classical course; the Philosophical course; and the Biblical course. Although differing in some respects, the aggregate of culture and instruction derived from each of these is supposed to be about equal in value. In addition to a very thorough academic course, preparatory to the above, there is also allowed to such students as are prepared to do so with advantage, the privilege of pursuing an Eclectic course. There is also established and maintained a Normal course to aid such students as desire to qualify themselves for the practical work of teaching. During the junior and senior years certain elective studies are allowed in all the courses. Great importance is attached to a thorough public examination of the pupils in all their studies. There is no charge for tuition in any department of the University. Ladies are admitted to all the classes and departments of the institution, and are allowed to graduate on the same terms as gentlemen. "In opposition to the cry of no religion in the schools," Asbury University adheres to the Christian religion as the very life and soul of all that is valuable in instruction and discipline.

The present Faculty consists of Alexander Martin, D. D., President, and Professor of Mental and Moral Science.

Joseph Tingley, Ph. D., Vice-President and Professor of Natural Science.

Philander Wiley, D. D., Professor of Greek Language and Literature.

Lewis L. Rogers, Ph. D., Professor of Latin Language and Literature.

John Clark Ridpath, A. M., Professor of Belles-lettres and History.

Rev. John E. Earp, A. M., Professor of Modern Languages and Hebrew.

Rev. Patterson McNutt, A. M., Professor of Mathematics.

Reuben Andrus, D. D., Professor of Biblical Literature.

John Brewer DeMotte, A. B., Principal of Preparatory Department, and Instructor of Mathematics.

EARLHAM COLLEGE.—Earlham College is located about one mile west of Richmond, on a tract of land containing 160 acres. The building, besides its halls, study-rooms, recitation-rooms, etc., affords accommodations for 180 students. The college was founded by "Indiana Yearly Meeting of Friends" (Orthodox), in 1847, with the title "Friends' Boarding School," which it retained till 1859. Said "Yearly Meeting," having been incorporated in 1850 for educational as well as religious purposes, in the year 1859 exercised its legal authority in changing the name of the institution to Earlham College, and authorized the faculty to confer degrees.

For several years the college was without a president. The first to occupy this office was Barnabas C. Hobbs, LL. D., who resigned to accept the office of State Superintendent of Public Instruction in 1868. He was succeeded by the present incumbent, Joseph Moore, A. M., who has held his office seven years. There is a preparatory school connected with the college. Two courses of study, a classical and a scientific course, are embraced in the curriculum. At present there are six professors. In the preparatory department there is a principal, with other efficient teachers. The adjuncts to the system of instruction in the college are: libraries containing over 4,000 volumes; a well stocked reading room; a museum arranged for instruction in mineralogy, geology, zoölogy, comparative anatomy, archæology and botany; a laboratory for students in chemical analysis; a collection of engineering and philosophical apparatus; and an astronomical observatory, furnished with a telescope, a transit instrument, and an astronomical clock.

Seventy-nine students, eighteen of whom are ladies, have graduated since the establishment of the college, with the degree of A. B. or B. S. Higher degrees have never been conferred "in course." The requirements for the degree of A. M. are such that but few graduates have yet made the effort necessary to obtain it. It is the determined purpose of the authorities that all diplomas and degrees shall be awarded only for real merit and solid attainments.

There is an endowment fund of $50,000. In accordance with the design of the founders of Earlham College, special attention is given to thoroughness in all the branches taught, and to the inculcation of moral and religious principles.

The present Faculty consists of Joseph Moore, A. M., President.

Eli Jay, A. M., Mental Philosophy and Geology.

William A. Moore, M. S., Mathematics.

Calvin W. Pearson, Ph. D., Modern Languages and History.

Alpheus McTaggart, A. B., Greek and Latin.

David W. Dennis, A. B., Chemistry.

William N. Trueblood, A. B., English Literature and Elocution.

Deborah A. Steere, B. S., Instructor in Botany.

Mahalah Jay, A.M., Principal of Preparatory Department.

Northwestern Christian University.—The charter of this institution is an act of the General Assembly of the State of Indiana, approved January 15, 1850. The act provides for the formation of a joint stock company with a capital stock of not less than $75,000 or more than $500,000, divided into shares of $100 each.

The objects of the incorporation, as expressed in the charter, were: "To found and sustain, at or in the vicinity of Indianapolis, an institution of learning of the highest class, for the education of youth; to establish in said institution colleges in every branch of liberal and professional education; to educate and prepare suitable teachers for the common schools; to teach and inculcate the Christian faith and morality as taught in the Sacred Scriptures, making those Scriptures the sole authoritative text-book in such instruction; and for the promotion of the sciences and arts."

The institution was located on a campus of twenty-five acres, then immediately adjoining the city of Indianapolis, now annexed to the city. Upon this campus a college building was erected at a cost of about $30,000. The institution was opened in this building in November, 1855, and was continued there until June, 1875. The increase in the value of the grounds belonging to the campus induced the desire to remove the institution, and make sale of the grounds for the purpose of increasing the endowment fund. Accordingly, the Board of Directors, July 24, 1873, accepted an offer, made by the citizens of Irvington and vicinity, of twenty-five acres of ground as a college campus, and notes and obligations for the payment of money, amounting in the aggregate to $150,000, as a *bonus* for the location. The institution was located upon the grounds so offered and accepted. They are situated about four miles east of Indianapolis. On this campus a good college building has been erected at a cost of some $60,000. It will accommodate five hundred students. The twenty-first session of the institution was opened in the new building, September 15, 1875.

Two-thirds of the capital stock of the corporation is set apart by the charter as an endowment fund. A course of Biblical study, in which the Bible is made the text-book, is included in the regular course of studies in the institution. Students of either sex are admitted to the University on equal terms.

Of the old campus, about six acres, including the ground upon which the old college building stands, are reserved. The building will probably be used in the future for colleges of Law and Medicine. The remainder of the property has been laid off in lots, the most of which have been sold, and three-fourths of the purchase money, outstanding in bonds and mortgages, has been added to the endowment fund.

The endowment fund of the institution now amounts to about $250,000.

Reserved portion of the old campus and building, $100,000.

The new campus and building, $100,000.

Other property and funds belonging to the building fund, $50,000.

Aggregate amount of property and funds belonging to the institution, $500,000.

Ovid Butler, LL. D., of Indianapolis, the chancellor, is the great benefactor of the institution. He originally donated the old campus, which at the time it was subdivided was worth about $350,000. At various other times, he has given large sums of money to relieve the institution. He has endowed a professorship called the "Demia Butler Chair of English Literature," in honor of his daughter Demia, now deceased, who was the first female graduate in the regular classical course of the college. The chair is to be perpetually filled by a lady, who is, in all respects, on an equality with the male professors.

The present Faculty consists of O. A. Burgess, President and Professor of Biblical Department and of Metaphysics.

W. M. Thrasher, Professor of Mathematics and Astronomy.

Scot Butler, Professor of Latin Language and Literature.

John O. Hopkins, Professor of Greek Language and Literature.

F. W. Achilles, Professor of Chemistry and Physiology; also German and French Languages.

D. S. Jordan, Professor of Natural History.

Miss Catharine Merrill, Professor of Demia Butler Chair of English Literature.

C. E. Hollenbeck, Professor of Commercial Department.

Isaac Errett, Lecturer on Homiletics.

S. K. Hoshour, Professor of Ecclesiastical History and Biblical Archaeology.

Purdue University.—Purdue University is the corporate name of the institution which represents the college originating in the act of Congress of July 2, 1862. The object of that act, as expressed by its title, was "to donate public lands to the several states and territories which may provide colleges for the benefit of agricultural and the mechanic arts." The act assumes to grant to each state an amount of public lands equal to thirty thousand acres for each of her senators and representatives in Congress. Indiana, having no public land within her borders, obtained her donation in scrip, amounting to 390,000 acres. March 6, 1865, the legislature of Indiana passed an act accepting the national donation, and organizing a board of trustees for the management of the trust funds, to be known as "The Trustees of the Indiana Agricultural College." This board was authorized to sell the land scrip allotted to the State. There was realized therefrom $212,238.50. This fund has accumulated until it now reaches about $365,000. It is invested in interest-bearing U. S. bonds. This, under the act of Congress, is purely an endowment fund. May 6, 1869, the legislature of Indiana accepted a donation of $150,000 from John Purdue; another of $50,000 from Tippecanoe County; and also one hundred acres of land from the citizens of Chauncey. The State has, since that time, appropriated $80,000 for building purposes. In consideration of the donations, the name was changed to "Purdue University," and the institution was located near Chauncey, a suburb of Lafayette, in Tippecanoe County. The landed possessions at this time consist of 186 acres; the buildings consist of a boarding-house, dormitory, laboratory, boiler and gas-house, all built of brick; a military hall and gymnasium, farm-house, barn, etc., built of wood.

A formal opening of the school was ordered for September 17, 1874, and on that day the first regular term began with the following faculty:

Abraham C. Shortridge, President; John S. Hougham, Professor of Physics; John Hussey, Botany and Horticulture; Wm. B. Morgan, Mathematics; Harvey W. Wiley, Chemistry; Eli F. Brown, English Literature and Drawing. At the close of the first year W. B. Morgan resigned; his place was afterward filled by David G. Herron. Prof. Hussey was transferred to the chair of Modern Languages, and Mrs. Sarah A. Oren was elected to the chair of Botany. President Shortridge resigned December 31, 1875, and Hon. E. E. White, of Ohio, was elected to fill the vacancy. The schools of the University are as follows: 1. School of Natural Sciences; 2. School of Engineering 3. School of Agriculture. Under these schools ther are regular courses in Agriculture and Horticulture, Civil Engineering, Mechanical Engineering, Mining Engineering, Industrial Design, Natural History, and Chemistry.

Since the opening of the University, it has been attended by about sixty students each year. Its prospects for the future are good. Its endowment fund more than pays its present faculty; its land and buildings, with the main building now in contemplation, will amply meet the wants of the institution. Its libraries and apparatus are being increased as demand is felt.

University of Notre Dame.—This institution is located at Notre Dame, near South Bend, and is under the control of the Roman Catholics. It was founded in 1842 by the congregation of the Holy Cross, under the direction of Very Rev. E. Sorin, and was chartered by the legislature of the State in 1844, with power to confer all the usual degrees. The college buildings are commodious, the grounds are tastefully arranged and well-kept, and the site is beautiful.

Some of the regulations, not common to other universities of the State, are as follows, viz.: "The use of tobacco is strictly forbidden to such as have not permission from their parents or guardians. No one shall leave the University grounds without permission from the president or vice-president. Students are expected to take baths regularly. No book, periodical, or newspaper shall be introduced into the college without being previously examined and approved by the director of studies. Objectionable books found in the possession of the students will be withheld from them until their departure from the university. All letters sent or received by students may be opened by the president or his representatives. Students are not allowed to keep money in their possession. Whatever pocket money parents may choose to allow their sons must be placed in the hands of the treasurer."

The college library contains about twelve thousand volumes. The number of students enrolled in the year ending June, '75, as shown by the catalogue, is 350. The whole number of graduates to the same date is 84. The founder of the University was the first president, and he continued in office for 23 years. Rev. P. J. Colovin, who was inaugurated in 1874, is now president.

St. Mary's Academy.—This school was chartered in 1855. It is under the direction of the sisters of the Holy Cross, and is situated one mile from Notre Dame University. It is under the same general control as the University, and is in reality a female branch of the same institution. The academy is in a flourishing condition. Mother M. Angela, Superior, has immediate charge.

Union Christian College.—The establishment of this college was proposed by Elder E. W. Humphrey, in the Western Indiana Christian Conference, in 1858. The name was suggested by Elder Abraham Sneathen. The location at Merom, Sullivan County, was made in consideration of a donation of $35,000, the superiority of the building site, and the remoteness of the place from competing colleges. The college building, 109 feet long, 69 feet broad, four stories high, including the basement, and costing $42,000, was dedicated December, 1862. Its endowment fund at present aggregates $100,000, yielding an annual income of $6,000. Its first president was N. Summerbell, D. D., who served as such from 1860 to 1865; its second, Thomas Holmes, D. D., from 1865 to 1875; its third, the present incumbent, Rev. T. C. Smith, A. M. It has a complete philosophical and chemical apparatus, a good geological cabinet, a library, and a reading-room. Two literary societies, each in its own well-furnished hall, hold weekly meetings.

Merom contains about six hundred inhabitants, and is situated upon a bluff two hundred feet above the waters of the Wabash and the prairies of Illinois beyond. Sullivan is the railroad station.

The college is under the control of the Christians (New Lights) who formulate their principles as follows:

1. The Bible,—the sufficient rule and creed.

2. Christian,—the proper and sufficient name.

3. Christian Character,—the sufficient test of church fellowship.

4. Liberty of conscience in all matters of disputed interpretation and opinion.

The courses of study—preparatory, scientific, and classical—are thorough and practical, and lay a good basis for any special course. The institution gives Christian, but not sectarian, instruction.

Franklin College.—This institution is situated at Franklin, Ind. It was founded in 1835, under the title

"Manual Labor Institute." Its origin was due to a deep conviction on the part of leading Indiana Baptists, that their denomination needed a school of higher learning in the State. Among the founders were Lewis Morgan, Henry Bradley, Samuel Harding, and Jesse Holman. In those early days men gave not only money, but also such goods as they could spare. Among the gifts made, the record mentions nails, leather, locks, cows, pigs, and clocks.

In 1844, the name was changed to Franklin College; college functions were assumed, and Rev. Geo. C. Chandler, of Indianapolis, was chosen president. He served ten years with ability. In 1853, Silas Bailey, D. D., of Granville, Ohio, was elected to the presidency. He was a man of learning and large sympathies, and exerted an influence for good throughout the State. During his administration an additional building was erected. Failing health compelled him to resign in 1863. He died in 1875, leaving to the college his library and a large portion of his estate.

The college suspended operations for several years during the war. In 1869, the board again assumed control, and elected a faculty with Rev. W. T. Stott as senior professor and acting president. In 1870, H. L. Wayland, D. D., of Kalamazoo, Mich., was elected president. He served nearly two years, when the embarrassed financial condition of the college led him to resign. In 1872, a new organization was effected, known as "Franklin College Association." The college under the new organization, with Rev. W. T. Stott as president, has had uniform success. The patronage has increased from twenty to thirty per cent each year, and an average of over *ten thousand dollars* per annum has been added to the endowment fund. The work of the class-room claims to be of a high character. One year has been added to the Preparatory Course, so that the curriculum of study is quite extensive.

In common with the Baptist schools of the entire country, Franklin is hoping much from the Centennial year.

The present assets, above all liabilities, are:

Grounds and Buildings . . .	$40,000
Library	2,000
Apparatus and Geological Cabinet .	1,000
Endowment Subscription . . .	85,000
Total	$128,000

There are also bequests made in favor of the college amounting to about $30,000.

Smithson College.—This institution had its origin in a small bequest of $8,000 made by Joshua Smithson of Switzerland County, to the Universalist denomination. It was located at Logansport, in consequence of a donation of $20,000 by Mrs. Elizabeth Holland, of that city. It has twelve acres of ground, is situated on a beautiful and commanding elevation on the north side of the Wabash River, overlooking the city and valley below. Its buildings, in point of appearance and arrangement, are models. It was designed for the joint occupancy of boarders and students of both sexes, and every part has relation to this purpose.

Judge Hervey Cravens is president, and Hon. W. W. Curry, secretary of the board of trustees. Its present faculty consists of Rev. R. N. John, A. M., acting president; Miss Leora E. Bowyer, lady principal;

Professors Lee, Baldwin, Hall, and Peakes; Miss Martin, teacher of music; Miss Justice, teacher of painting. It has no endowment, and depends on current receipts for expenses.

De Pauw Female College.—This college is situated at New Albany. The building was originally erected in 1853, under the direction of the Indiana conference of the M. E. Church. A few years ago, Mr. De Pauw endowed the institution with considerable funds, after which the east wing was erected, completing the building as originally designed. The entire cost was about $35,000. The college has for the past six years been under the charge of President Erastus Rowley. March 8, 1876, a fire injured thc building to the amount of some $10,000, which was fully covered by insurance.

Spiceland Academy.—Spiceland Academy was established in 1862, by Clarkson Davis, who was principal until 1866. The year 1866, Mr. Davis spent in Europe, and during his absence Edward Taylor, a graduate of Earlham College, acted as principal. After his return, Clarkson Davis was at the head of the academy until 1872, when he was succeeded by Timothy Wilson, who has remained in charge up to the present time. The institution was incorporated in 1871, and is controlled by six trustees, two of whom are chosen each year by Spiceland Monthly Meeting of Friends. The total enrollment for the year closing June, 1875, was 506. The course of study and the character of instruction entitle this academy to a place among the higher institutions of the State.

Moore's Hill College.—This college is located at Moore's Hill, in Dearborn County. It has been in operation for twenty years. The nineteenth catalogue, which is for the years '74 and '75, gives a summary of students enrolled for the college year as follows:

College Department	36
Preparatory Department	92
Musical Department	31
Total	159
Counted twice	18
Actual attendance	141

The classical course covers four years; the scientific course, three years. The whole number of classical graduates is 18, and of scientific graduates, 65. F. A. Hester, D. D., president, and three professors, constitute the faculty.

Hartsville University.—This institution, situated at Hartsville, Bartholomew County, is under the control of the United Brethren. It has but a small endowment, and consequently labors under some pecuniary embarrassment; nevertheless a faculty, consisting of a president and five professors and teachers is sustained, and the school has a good name. The classical course, which covers four years, includes the usual college work. The school was established in 1850, and the first class was graduated in 1859. The whole number of graduates is 37. The catalogue for 1874–5 shows the enrollment for the year to be in the college department—7 classical students and 35 scientific students. The number in all the departments is 159. Rev. W. J. Pruner is president.

REFORMATORY AND BENEVOLENT INSTITUTIONS.

BY

OTIS A. BURGESS, A. M.

REFORMATORY AND BENEVOLENT INSTITUTIONS.

AMONG the things most noteworthy which distinguish modern from ancient civilizations, may be mentioned Reformatory and Benevolent Institutions. Under the benign influences of the Christian religion, humanity is gradually approaching the grand idea of a common brotherhood; and the regulations of civil and social life, by a moral force more irresistible than the tread of martial hosts, are rapidly adapting themselves to the broad and generous impulses of the better nature of man. Under these impulses, the aged, the poor, the unfortunate, the decrepit, and the fallen, are no longer left homeless or destitute, much less put to death as the shortest mode of ridding them of their trouble and society of their presence; but they are provided with homes, houses of refuge, hospitals, and asylums, some of which are founded and maintained, regardless of cost and trouble, by the State, while others are the fruits of that pure Christian charity and benevolence which seek to reduce to real life the golden rule.

Indiana, in her public character, and in her private

benevolent enterprises will compare, not unfavorably, with her sister States.

The following statement will show as fully as practicable in the space allotted to this chapter, the general scope and intent of the various local charitable institutions of Indianapolis, and of Marion County, both public and private. These are selected for description, because they may be taken as institutions typical of those which are to be found in almost every city and county in the State. The statement also describes the work of the State Benevolent and Reformatory Institutions.

The Marion County Infirmary.—This institution was founded as early as 1832, and is situated about three miles north-west of Indianapolis. A farm consisting of 160 acres was purchased at the time mentioned. The only building then upon it was a log cabin of two rooms. Other buildings have been erected from time to time as the wants of the institution have demanded, until, at present, there are ample and commodious rooms to meet all usual requirements. The main building is 204 by 184 feet, four stories high, and was erected at a cost of $120,000. Separate and convenient apartments are provided for the sexes, and the institution is under the best of management. The physician-in-chief receives but a moderate salary for his services, and his work may really be styled a work of charity. Nearly 200 inmates have been provided for within the space of a single year. Almost all conditions of society and of disease that properly come under the care of the county authorities are found in this institution.

The City Hospital.—This institution takes rank among the most worthy of the benevolent enterprises of Indianapolis. It was established in March, 1856, by the Common Council of the City, and the buildings were completed in 1859. This institution, of which Indiana may be justly proud, has conferred an inestimable boon upon the poor and unfortunate. Nearly 2,000 patients have been treated since the erection of the buildings. An average of thirty is constantly under treatment in the institution. The average number of cures has been large, which speaks volumes for the care and skill of the attending physicians.

THE INDIANAPOLIS BENEVOLENT SOCIETY.—This society was organized on the Thanksgiving evening of November, 1835, a fit occasion for so noble a work. The movement was participated in by the churches of Indianapolis, irrespective of denominational lines; and each Thanksgiving evening, from the date of organization until the present time, has been sacredly observed by the churches in a union meeting, held to devise plans for carrying forward the good work. As the name indicates, it is a purely benevolent work; there are no salaried officers and no paid agents. Each year the city is divided into small districts. A committee of one lady and one gentleman is appointed for each district. The whole city is thus thoroughly canvassed. Contributions of money, food, or clothing are solicited from all who are able to contribute, and the names and the residences of those who in any manner need aid are taken. These committees report to head-quarters, depositing with the proper officers their collections, and whenever a call is made for aid, the books are at once consulted to ascertain whether the name and residence of the applicant have been taken by the canvassers; if there be doubt as to the genuineness of the claim, a committee at once visits the residence of the claimant, making personal inspection of the case. Thus, very few worthy objects of charity are passed by unaided, and very few unworthy persons impose upon the benevolence of the people. By these means also, public begging from house to house is almost entirely prevented, and the visitor to the capital often remarks the freedom of the city from street beggars. It would be impossible to estimate the amount of suffering alleviated and exposure avoided, through the aid of this truly Christian institution.

THE LADIES' SOCIETY FOR THE RELIEF OF THE POOR. —This society was organized in February, 1869, by Protestant and Catholic ladies. It has, on the one hand, the laudable desire to overcome all denominational differences in the great work of benevolence, and on the other, the work of cultivating that spirit of charity which thinketh no evil. It has proved itself a helpful auxiliary in the good work of stimulating the benevolent activities of those with whom its members are associated.

THE ORPHANS' HOME.—Perhaps no appeal more touching or tender comes to the human heart, than that made by the mute lips and pale face of a little parentless child. The women, always in some good work—"last at the cross and first at the tomb"—have not passed that appeal by. The Orphans' Home was chartered in 1850. From time to time, suitable buildings have been erected, and the Home, under the judicious management of devoted Christian women, has been a home indeed for many an orphan wanderer that might otherwise have perished on the streets, or have found its way into those dens of infamy where so many unfortunates barter away character and soul for a scanty and wretched subsistence. The number of inmates varies from 50 to 100 per year. At present there are 75. These little waifs are cared for with the watchfulness of a mother's love, and as soon as possible they are placed in families where they may receive the advantages of a good and permanent home.

HOME FOR FRIENDLESS WOMEN.—This institution is located near the city limits. The name sufficiently explains the intent of its founding. A home is provided for those women who are destitute of home and friends. Not only are the fallen cared for, but the needy and unfortunate are also received without regard to the cause of their misfortune.

It was opened in February, 1867, and had 70 inmates the first year. The number has increased from year to year, reaching at times nearly 300.

Its management has been upon a careful and economical basis, and the good results both to the inmates and to society at large are manifest.

INDIANAPOLIS ASYLUM FOR FRIENDLESS COLORED CHILDREN.—This institution was established in 1870, and is located in the north-western part of the city. Recognizing the voice of Him who said "of one blood have I made all nations," the movement was inaugurated the more effectively to care for those poor waifs thrown helplessly upon society, whose condition was all the more pitiable on account of that wicked prejudice against color. In this institution the poor colored child receives the same attention as though his face were of the fairest hue. A benevolence is surely sincere when the most stubborn prejudices are overcome in order to display it.

There are in addition to the above named societies and institutions other local associations, such as the German Protestant, and Ladies' German Protestant, Aid Societies; societies for the relief of the crippled and deformed; private institutions of charity; free medical dispensaries, etc., etc., all of which are working in the same general channels of charity, benevolence, and reform, and are accomplishing incalculable good for every class of sufferers by misfortune as well as by crime.

INDIANA HOUSE OF REFUGE.—This institution was founded in March, 1867, and opened January, 1868. It is located near Plainfield. The Assembly that authorized its establishment appropriated $50,000 to carry out the provisions of the act. The buildings and grounds cost $180,000. The institution seeks to reform "juvenile offenders." There were 112 inmates the first year, and the total number admitted to date is 720.

The general scope of the training and instruction is to reform, rather than punish, and to reclaim to the walks of good society those youths who otherwise would grow up in the school of crime. Good results have constantly flowed from this fountain of benevolence.

INDIANA INSTITUTE FOR THE DEAF AND DUMB.—This institution, located near Indianapolis, was authorized by an act of the General Assembly in 1844. Buildings large and commodious have been erected, showing a front of 260 feet, and a depth of 80 feet. These are three stories high, and cost not far from $225,000.

There are connected with this institution over 100 acres of ground, which, owing to its nearness to the city, is worth not less than $2,000 per acre. The annual appropriation for the maintenance of the institution by the State is about $45,000.

The attendance of pupils ranges from two hundred to three hundred each year.

As this is an institute of learning, and not an asylum, all the means and facilities requisite thereto are brought to bear on the question of educating the inmates.

Only those who have been engaged in the education of the deaf mute can understand the difficulties attending such a work, especially in the case of those born deaf and dumb. To substitute signs physical for signs vocal, and to arouse the understanding and reason to the proper significance of the world without and the *self* within, is a work of no small magnitude. Step by step and year by year, however, have these difficult tasks been performed, and with such marked success that the visitor to the institute carries away the impression that the "poor unfortunates" are about the merriest people of earth. Indiana has reason to be proud of the success of this institution.

THE INDIANA INSTITUTE FOR THE EDUCATION OF THE BLIND.—This State Institution was founded by an act of the General Assembly in 1847, and was opened in October of the same year. The present buildings, most beautifully situated on the north side and near mid-way east and west of the original town-plat of Indianapolis, were erected at a cost of about $100,000; the buildings with the grounds, at this date, are probably worth three or four times that amount. They present a frontage of 150 feet, with an average depth of about 90 feet; the center is five, and the wings are four stories high. There are ample accommodations for a large class of pupils, and every appliance that modern benevolence can suggest or modern skill contrive, has been brought into requisition for the benefit of this unfortunate class of our fellow-beings.

The first year there were received for education 25 pupils. From that date to the present, the entire number received is 521,—283 males and 238 females.

The institution has two departments—the school and the industrial. In the former the following branches are taught: orthography, reading, writing, English grammar, rhetoric, composition, arithmetic, algebra, physical and descriptive geography, history, physiology, anatomy, botany, mental moral and natural philosophy, and vocal and instrumental music.

In the Industrial Department, the males make brooms and brushes of all kinds, carpets, mats, chairs, and baskets. The females make aprons, bed comforts, spreads and ticks, handkerchiefs, towels, table covers, and a great variety of ladies' wearing apparel, together with all kinds of bead and fancy work. The cost of maintaining the institution varying but little from $20,000 a year, is the merest trifle, while the amount of good accomplished in sending out young men and women well prepared to earn a competence, instead of being a perpetual charge to their friends, or beggars for daily food, is inestimable.

About three miles west of Indianapolis is situated THE INDIANA HOSPITAL FOR THE INSANE.—Perhaps no calamity of earth, except loss of character, is so great, so dreadful, as the loss of reason. If, therefore, it lies within the bounds of human possibility either to ameliorate the condition of the insane or to effect their cure, surely, a supreme endeavor—only to be surpassed in the effort to save the soul—should be put forth in their behalf. Thoroughly has Indiana appreciated this work, and nobly has she responded to its demands.

The Hospital for the Insane was founded by an act of the Assembly in 1847, and was opened for patients in 1848. The number of inmates the first year was: males 53, and females 51. The whole number admitted to October 31, 1875, was—males, 3231; females, 2981; total, 6212. The number in the Hospital, at this date, is 300 men and 300 women. Of the whole number treated, the per cent of deaths has been: males, 11.08; females, 9.76. Of those treated, the per cent cured is: males, 50.08; females, 48.87.

The present buildings show a front of 624 feet, the center being five, and the wings four stories high. They have a capacity for 500 patients. Connected with the buildings are 160 acres of ground, now of great value. These buildings were erected at a cost of $500,000. Insanity, however, being a malady that does not necessarily shorten life, and one certainly not easily cured, though the above per cent of cures speaks well for the skill of the attending physicians, it has been found necessary to enlarge the facilities for taking care of this class, and the State accordingly made liberal appropriations therefor. New buildings are now in process of erection, and it is supposed that they will be completed within two years. They will have a capacity for 600 additional patients. These buildings, when completed, will be occupied exclusively by the females, and the present structures will be occupied by the males exclusively. In the adaptation of the new buildings to the exact purposes for which they were designed, and in respect to modern appliances for comfort and convenience, it is perhaps not too much to say that no State will surpass Indiana. In prompt and efficient attention to the unfortunate that need public aid, she certainly stands in the front rank.

THE INDIANA SOLDIERS' HOME.—When patriotism dies, a nation is lost. Next to our God and his worship, must stand our country and her defenders; to provide, therefore, for those disabled in defense of the national life, and for the children of those brave men who have laid down their lives on the bloody field, is but the dictate of an impulse akin to worship itself. Indiana has not failed to recognize her duty to her living heroes or to the children of her dead.

The Indiana Soldiers' Home was established immediately after the close of the war. The Indianapolis city hospital building was occupied for this purpose from August, 1865, to April, 1866, during which time about 50 disabled soldiers were admitted. In the spring of 1866, the directors purchased the present site, known as Knightstown Springs, at Knightstown, to which place the Home was removed. Up to 1867, it was sustained by gifts and donations, obtained from all parts of the State. In 1867, it was recognized by the General Assembly, an appropriation being made of $50,000 for buildings; the words "and Sailors' and Orphans'" were added to the name, and it thus became one of Indiana's permanent benevolent institutions, to remain as long as the survivors of the war shall need its aid. The building was erected at a cost of something over $50,000. It is 150 by 60 feet, three stories high, and contains 48 rooms, each 23 by 16 feet, besides two large attic halls. It was occupied by the soldiers in June, 1868. During that year, 200 soldiers and 75 orphans were received. From year to year, however, the number of the soldiers so rapidly decreased, that it was deemed best to transfer the few remaining ones to the National Asylum, at Dayton, Ohio. Meantime, also, the number of orphans rapidly increased, so that all the accommodations were needed for them. There are now in the Home 250 children between the ages of six and fifteen. These children are provided for at the expense of the State; a good common school education is given them, and they are taught in the ways of uprightness and truth. If "the bones of the dead stir in the grave," it surely must be something of a balm to our fallen heroes that their children are being provided for at the hands of the State for whose glory they fell.

INDIANA FEMALE PRISON AND REFORMATORY.—No philanthropist has ever visited prisons who has not had occasion to lament over the defects of the prison system. If men and women must be deprived of their liberty for the good of society, it does not follow that they, even in prison walls, should be treated inhumanly, or even carelessly. The good people of Indiana, appreciating these things, began the agitation of the question of prison reform in 1869. The following are some of the results. Near Indianapolis has been erected a building 174 by 109 feet, as a main building, with wings to be extended, making an entire front of 575 feet.

The objects of this truly benevolent and philanthropic movement are, first, to hold in confinement that class of females so lost to self respect as to need compulsory seclusion from society; and, second, to reform those who are yet within the reach of good influence and example. Misfortune, poverty, the wiles of the seducer, rather than the mere desire for sensual indulgence, are often the causes of the first downward step to ruin; and such unfortunates, taken timely under protection from further temptations, may be restored to self respect and a useful life. The institution is accomplishing its purposes in a marked degree, and the State has reason to be proud of the humane influences here at work.

CONCLUSION.—More and more, year by year, are the people of Indiana awakening to the necessity of providing for all who need aid, and as far as possible, of removing the source whence acts of lawlessness and crime are continually flowing. Let it be hoped that those who celebrate the next centennial of American freedom and of American greatness, will find that the sword has not only been beaten into plowshares and the spear into pruning-hooks, but that jails and prisons have been turned into school-houses and churches, and men have ceased to study war and crime.

WOMEN IN THE SCHOOLS.

BY

GEORGE P. BROWN.

WOMEN IN THE SCHOOLS.

FIFTY, or even twenty-five years ago, the Hoosier school-master was a man. He was selected quite as much for his physical prowess as for his intellectual attainments. If he was able to read, write, and cipher, and to whip the largest boys, he was considered well qualified for his work. Women were seldom employed except in the cities, and then only in the primary schools. Ere long, however, it began to be manifest that love and kindness were much more potent elements than force in the management of the school, and from that time woman began to occupy a prominent place in the profession.

To write the history of woman's work in our public schools, is to write the history of nearly all that is valuable in them. Little has been accomplished in the immediate work of the school-room that is not the result of her labor. Her supremacy in the primary school is universally acknowledged, and she gives a character to much of the work in the higher departments.

Whether this is altogether wise or not, whether pupils would not leave school with minds more symmetrically developed, and in every way better prepared for life's duties, if they received more of their training from men, is a question worthy of serious consideration; but it is a question which it is not the province of this chapter to discuss. The proposition, however, is self-evident to those who have given the subject any considerable thought, that women possessing the high order of intellect, and the culture that most of our lady teachers do possess, are far superior as educators in every department to men of second or third rate ability. Until, therefore, the inducements for men to enter the profession of teaching shall equal those that now impel them to prepare for other vocations, the instruction in our schools will be delegated largely to women.

Many male teachers are employed in the rural districts throughout the State, but these are generally young men who are using the public school as a ladder by which they may climb to some profession more desirable. Since many vocations open to men are practically closed against women, either because of their nature, or of the custom that debars women from entering them, there is more inducement for young ladies, desiring to avoid a life of dependence, to prepare themselves thoroughly for the business of teaching. As a result, our schools are indebted largely to women for the success of most of the reforms and improvements that have been introduced in recent years. Woman's influence in the primary department during the last twenty years has worked a radical change in the methods of instruction and government in the schools throughout the State. Experienced and successful teachers, some with and many without Normal School training, have practically mastered both the science and art of teaching. They have devoted themselves to the study of the laws of mental growth, and by the aid of professional books and intelligent experiments, they have determined the course of study and a method of procedure, adapted to the needs of the child in his various stages of development.

The reforms, inaugurated and pursued so successfully in the lower grades, have suggested new methods in respect to the work in the higher grades. In studying to know what is best for the child and why it is best, the work and methods adapted to more mature minds have been discovered.

In reviewing the history of the progress of the reform in our elementary schools, it is seen to have commenced in the larger cities. Richmond, Fort Wayne, Indianapolis, Terre Haute, Lafayette, Evansville, and a few other towns became centers from which the surrounding country caught the spirit of the work, and to which the teachers in smaller towns and rural districts looked for instruction. The most rapid advance has been made within the last ten years. Previous to 1865, the public school term did not continue longer than from three to five months each year in most of the towns and cities of the State. This was too short a time for any thing but the most superficial work. Immediately, however, upon the re-enactment of the law providing for local taxation, all the principal cities extended their school term to ten months in the year, and thus made it possible to adopt and pursue a systematic course of instruction. Some of those who were most prominent in the primary work of former years have either withdrawn from the ranks, or have entered higher departments of the school. Among those who have been prominent in bringing to its present state of excellence our primary work are Amanda P. Funnelle, now teacher in the State Normal School; Nebraska Cropsey and Anna Barbour, of Indianapolis; Ruth Morris and Julia Test, of Richmond; and Mary H. Swan, Miss Lena Funnelle, and Miss Kittie Drake, of Fort Wayne.

But woman's field of labor is not confined to the primary grades, as the large number of women employed in our grammar and high schools attests. The improvements that have been made in the instruction in these departments are not so marked as in the lower schools for the following reasons:

1st. The work in the higher departments of school is not that for which woman is by nature so eminently fitted. 2d. The reform was commenced later, and teachers have not yet learned to adapt their instruction to that stage of mental growth in which it is necessary to blend, so to speak, the concrete and the abstract. One of these methods is apt to prevail too much to the exclusion of the other. In the department of English language, our lady teachers have commenced some much-needed reforms, and are prosecuting them with an intelligence and skill unsurpassed. Miss Mary Bruce, teacher of Language in the State Normal School, has prepared a course of study in this subject for that institution that for logical thought and arrangement is unequaled by any thing that has yet been presented to the public. Miss Ruth Morris, teacher of English in the Indianapolis High School, has taken up the same line of thought, and is adapting it successfully to the needs of the grammar and high school grades. Several other women are pursuing the same line of study, and are working with an energy and intelligence that shows clearly that the power of abstract reasoning and generalization is not limited to men. Among those who have been or are now prominent instructors in the higher departments of school work may be mentioned, in addition to those already named: Fidelia Anderson, Emily Johnson, Mary Nicholson, Mary McGregory, Rhoda Driggs, May W. Thompson, Ellen F. Thompson, Emma A. Greene, S. M. Lovejoy, Eliza F. Ford, and Mrs. N. A. Stone, of the Indianapolis High School; C. D. Fuller and S. B. Fowler, of Fort Wayne; Mrs. I. G. Holcomb, of Richmond; Mrs. D. B. Wells, of Plymouth; Miss Mary Reid, Frank Kendall, and Mrs. Barnes, of Madison; Mrs. Hunt, of Spencer; Mrs. H. S. McRae, Muncie; Mrs. S. Cox, Kokomo; Mrs. George Hufford, New Castle; Miss M. E. Lyon, La Porte; Miss Lydia Dimon, Attica; Sarah A. Oren, of Purdue University.

Judging from the immediate past, and the general satisfaction with the results achieved, it seems evident that the "Hoosier School-masters" of the immediate future will be women. The alluring possibilities of wealth and position which a rapidly developing State offers to men in other fields of labor, and the eminent success that woman has achieved in teaching, will cause her to be regarded for some years as the party best fitted to instruct children and youth. Subsequently, it will be discovered that both women and men have each a well-defined work to do which can not be delegated to the other without serious injury to the general good.

THE IDEA OF A NORMAL SCHOOL.

BY

WILLIAM A. JONES, A. M.

THE IDEA OF A NORMAL SCHOOL.

THE POPULAR IDEA.—Webster defines a Normal School to be "a school whose methods of instruction are to serve as a model for imitation; an institution for the education of teachers."

An institution, then, in which students are trained to *imitate* methods of teaching by which themselves are taught, is the idea of a Normal School set forth in the definition.

The definition is the *repository* of the thought of the people in regard to the object defined.

The fact that there is a growing demand for teachers who have had some special training in methods of teaching, has led some schools, established primarily for other purposes, to adopt the name *Normal School.* Others have added to their field of work a *Normal Department.*

The ends sought in these schools are a somewhat more careful study of the branches which the student is to teach, and some training in the details of school organization and school management. The methods of instruction under which the student prosecutes his work are supposed to be worthy of imitation.

These *best methods* are often settled by vote of

the class, irrespective of the nature of the subject of study, and of the law of mental development.

In this way, the thought of a normal school expressed in the definition quoted, is perpetuated. And a normal school is, in the thought of the people, a school whose methods of teaching are to serve as a model for imitation. Occasionally a student of superior endowments and unusual insight, breaks loose from the *best methods*, stops thinking the opinions of others, and thinks for himself. He finds the true method determined in the subject itself, and in the law of his own mind. He condemns normal schools as technical and pedantic. He achieves success as a teacher, not by imitation—not by following the popular idea of a normal school, but by violating it.

To imitate is a mechanical process. Doubtless it is better to *imitate* a good method in teaching, one which has been determined by principles and processes of which the imitator is unconscious, than to work without a method.

To imitate is a characteristic of the Chinese intellect, and of Chinese civilization. To imitate is childish; it is spiritually dwarfing; it is deadening to all free activity. So far as it involves intellectual activity, it is thinking others' opinions—it is thinking by authority. It is technical. It is pedantic. There is in it no inspiration for either teacher or scholar.

THE TRUE IDEA.—Every object of our investigation, whether it belong to the world of matter or of mind, if it be a whole in itself, has a purpose, and the object exists for the realization of its purpose. Such an object exists for itself—has its own purpose within itself, which makes it to be what it is. A part of such object does not exist for itself, but for the whole. It can be understood only in relation to the whole. A plant is a whole. Its purpose is to reproduce itself. The process and mode of its development point to this end. Its purpose determines the order and mode of its growth. When we know the order, the mode of development, and the purpose of the plant, we understand it as an object existing for itself; when we study the plant as a relative object, we study the conditions essential to its growth, on the one side, and the related purposes of its growth—food for animals, etc.—on the other. To know the plant as a *man* knows it, not as a beast, one must know its purpose; the mode by which it attains its purpose as a being existing for itself; the conditions of its growth, and the purposes which it subserves as a related being. In general, if the object of study be one of nature, it contains its purpose within itself, and its purpose determines the order and mode by which the purpose realizes itself. If the object of study be a mechanism, as a table or a steam-engine, it still has its purpose, but the purpose is put into table or engine by the mechanic.

If the object of study be a work of art, as a statue, a painting, or a poem, it still has a purpose, but the purpose was put into the object by the artist. Every human institution has a purpose, and the purpose is put into the institution by those who form it. The purpose is a thought in the mind of mechanic, artist, or citizen. The purpose determines the process of construction—the selection, arrangement, and adaptation of parts.

Neither the machine, nor the work of art, nor the institution, is understood in any intelligent sense till its purpose is known, the relation of the parts to one another and to the whole, and the mode by which the whole accomplishes its purpose.

Every object in nature, every object of man's creation embodies thought. Things symbolize thought. The mind of every person is challenged to interpret the thought in things.

In the order of creation in nature, and of construction by man, the thought or purpose comes first; the object through or by means of which the purpose becomes an objective fact, last. In the order of our investigation the objective fact comes first, the purpose last. By the law of intellectual development we are required to begin with the object as a sensuous fact, and proceed from this to the thought in the object, and to the relations which it involves.

These two—the thought in the thing, and the law in the mind—are the elements which determine a natural and universal method of teaching. A method determined by any other conditions must be, in the nature of the case, factitious and partial.

The method above described is characterized as the *natural* one.

Whether the subject of study or of instruction be an object of nature or a human production, it is a thing existing independent of myself. The thought which it expresses exists independent of my thought. I am to find my way to the thought in the thing, and interpret it to myself. Or, having done this, I am to lead another to do the same thing for himself—*to teach him.*

The thought in the thing, and the method of realizing the thought, I can have no influence over. These are fixed. Even my own mind—the investigating and interpreting agent—is itself an object of nature. It contains within itself its own purpose and mode or law of action by which this purpose can be attained. These facts I can not change. But in the latter case the *self*, the interpreting agent, is endowed with the wonderful power of making its own activities the objects of its investigations.

It can infer—or better, *see* the purpose of its own existence, and know the method of its own spontaneous activity. It can direct and energize these activities only in accordance with the laws of its own being, for the realization of its purpose.

One can put no *new* faculty into his spirit; he can only develop by exercise such as are already there by nature.

Hence, the law of his own mind, when consciously apprehended, enables one to give intelligent direction to the method of his investigation, and of his instruction.

Since neither the thought in the thing nor the law in the mind is under the control of the investigator or of the teacher, but both exist independent of his will, the method determined by them must be the natural one. It is universal because it is natural.

Such method is not settled by the authority of opinions. It is settled by no association, or institute, or school. It is settled by the Creator himself.

The fact in the thing, and the law in the mind determine the method.

The true work of a Normal School, then, is: first, to train its students to such habits of thought and methods of investigation, as will enable them to determine for themselves the boundaries of each subject which they are to teach, to determine its content or subject-matter, to determine the logical dependence of the parts of the subject, and to determine the relation of the whole to other subjects.

This process is finding "the fact in the thing."

Second, to lead its students to study the forms and order of the spontaneous activity of their own minds. From such study one may gain a knowledge of the laws of his own spiritual activity and of the purposes of his different faculties and powers. This knowledge enables one to direct intelligently his activities in the mastery of a subject of study.

It enables him to know when he has "thought the subject." It aids him in the conduct of his personal culture. It aids him in the formation of his own character. This knowledge enables one to direct the efforts of those whom he shall teach to the same ends. This knowledge is what is meant by "knowledge of the law in the mind." These two knowledges are necessary to the teacher; for, in the presentation of a subject to children, what is first in the order of necessity and of logical dependence, is last in the order of apprehension by the child. What is first in the order of his cognition is last in the order of logical dependence. Having the two knowledges, knowledge of the subject and knowledge of the mind, the teacher can distinguish between the logical and the chronological order of presentation. He can choose either, according to the purpose he has in view and the state of mind of the learner. A teacher thus trained, can never be satisfied to be a mere imitator. He can never become mechanical, technical, deadening in his teaching. Penetrated with this idea, mastery of the subject and mastery of himself, he can never be a superficial person, never a superficial teacher. He alone can *simplify* truth and present it according to the capacity of the learner. He only can distinguish between the important and the unimportant. He only can teach *truly* the most in the shortest time.

Third, A person may possess the two knowledges described, and yet fail to be an efficient practical teacher. With these acquirements, one may determine theoretically, *what* should be taught, and *how* it should be taught, but fail in the actual practice of teaching.

A third and important part of Normal School work is training in the practice of teaching till the pupil-teacher acquires a reasonable degree of skill in the art. Thus, Normal School work presents three essential phases of culture and training.

THE PRESENT SYSTEM,

(WITH STATISTICAL TABLES.)

BY

JAMES. H. SMART, A.M.

THE PRESENT SYSTEM.

THE school system of Indiana is the result of a growth of less than twenty-five years. The few common schools scattered over the State prior to the adoption of the new constitution in 1852, mainly dependent as they were upon local voluntary enterprise, formed in no sense a State system. The people were permitted to open and maintain schools, but they were not compelled to do so. No State tax was levied, and no officers were made responsible to the State for the establishment and supervision of a general system of schools which should be supported by all and should be open to all. The framers of the new constitution, realizing that knowledge and virtue are the chief corner stones of a free republic, laid the foundations of our present system so broad and so deep that its perpetuity is placed beyond question. The following are the CONSTITUTIONAL PROVISIONS upon which the system is based:

SECTION 1. Knowledge and learning, generally diffused throughout a community, being essential to the preservation of a free government, it shall be the duty of the General Assembly to encourage, by all suitable means, moral, intellectual, scientific, and agricultural improvement, and to provide, by law, for a general and uniform system of common schools, wherein tuition shall be without charge, and equally open to all.

SEC. 2. The common school fund shall consist of the Congressional township fund, and the lands belonging thereto;

The Surplus Revenue fund;

The Saline fund and the lands belonging thereto;

The Bank Tax fund, and the fund arising from the one hundred and fourteenth section of the charter of the State Bank of Indiana;

The fund to be derived from the sale of county seminaries, and the moneys and property heretofore held for such seminaries; from the fines assessed for breaches of the penal laws of the State, and from all forfeitures which may accrue;

All lands and other estate which shall escheat to the State for want of heirs or kindred entitled to the inheritance;

All lands that have been, or may hereafter be, granted to the State, where no special purpose is expressed in the grant, and the proceeds of the sales thereof, including the proceeds of the sales of the swamp lands granted to the State of Indiana by the act of Congress of the 28th September, 1850, after deducting the expense of selecting and draining the same;

Taxes on the property of corporations, that may be assessed for common school purposes.

SEC. 3. The principal of the common school fund shall remain a perpetual fund, which may be increased, but shall never be diminished; and the income thereof shall be inviolably appropriated to the support of common schools, and to no other purpose whatever.

SEC. 4. The General Assembly shall invest, in some safe and profitable manner, all such portions of the common school fund as have not hereintofore been intrusted to the several counties; and shall make provision by law for the distribution, among the several counties, of the interest thereof.

SEC. 5. If any county shall fail to demand its proportion of such interest, for common school purposes, the same shall be re-invested for the benefit of such county.

SEC. 6. The several counties shall be held liable for the preservation of so much of the said fund as may be intrusted to them, and for the payment of the annual interest thereon.

SEC. 7. All trust funds, held by the State, shall remain inviolate, and be faithfully and exclusively applied to the purposes for which the trust was created.

SEC. 8. The General Assembly shall provide for the election, by the voters of the State, of a State Superintendent of Public Instruction, who shall hold his office for two years, and whose duties and compensation shall be prescribed by law.

From the date of the adoption of these fundamental laws, the growth of the school system has been very rapid.

A large school fund has been created and made productive; a grand system has been organized and perfected; public sentiment has been aroused and molded aright; school-houses have been built by the thousand; schools have been opened within convenient distance of almost every child in the State; cities and villages have maintained high schools and training schools; a State Normal School has been established; colleges and universities have been founded, and the whole educational machinery of the State has been admirably adjusted and adapted to the wants of a great commonwealth.

A comparative statement of a few leading facts will bring into contrast the condition of things as it existed twenty-five years ago, and as it is to-day. Then the length of school was but fifty days, now schools continue in session one hundred and thirty days: then the school-master was often sought from afar, to-day thirteen thousand men and women adorn their profession, honoring themselves and the State alike; then the school-houses were few in number and inferior in character, to-day there are ten thousand, most of them tasteful and convenient, and many of them models of elegance; then there was spent, for all purposes, less than half a million of dollars annually, to-day we pay nearly three millions of dollars to teachers alone, and two millions more for special purposes; then the value of the school property was scarcely worth estimating, to-day we have school property, in addition to the fund, to the amount of ten millions of dollars, devoted exclusively to educational purposes; then the number of children enrolled in the schools was but a handful, to-day a grand army of more than half a million enroll themselves as pupils; then the common school fund was but two and a half millions, to-day it aggregates eight and three-quarter millions. Above all these evidences of prosperity, and far better than any of them, are those results which can be estimated only by measuring the intelligence and the culture of the people.

THE LAW WHICH GOVERNS THE SYSTEM.—The following condensed statement of the powers and duties of the school officers will give, in brief outline, the main features of the school system of the State.

THE STATE SUPERINTENDENT OF PUBLIC INSTRUCTION is a constitutional officer, and is elected by the qualified voters of the State at a general election, for a term of two years. He is charged with the administration of the system of public instruction, with the general superintendence of the business relating to the common schools of the State and with the supervision of the school funds and revenues, appropriated for their support. It is his duty to render an opinion, in writing, to any school officer, so desiring, in regard to the administration or construction of the school law; he must also visit every county in the State, at least once in two years, and examine the Auditor's books and records, relative to the disposition of the school funds, the character of the loans made, and the manner in which the school revenues are collected and distributed. He must confer with the school officers, counsel with the teachers, and make public addresses as occasion may require. He is required to keep the general account of the school funds. To enable him to do this the county officers report to him, in June of each year, a detailed statement of the amount of funds on hand at the date of the last report, the additions made thereto, during the year, and the condition of the loans. This report forms the basis of the annual settlement between the counties and the State. He receives from the County Auditors semi-annual statements of the amount of State school tax collected, the amount of interest received on the fund held in trust by the counties, etc., and the reports of the manner in which the County Auditors have made the semi-annual distribution of school revenues to the various school corporations. These transactions are more fully explained under the head of school revenues. He receives statistical reports from the county superintendents, of various kinds, and apportions the State school revenue for tuition to the various counties, in proportion to the number of school children in each.

The State Superintendent hears appeals from the decisions of the county superintendents, in certain cases of general importance, including the granting of a license to a teacher and the revoking of the same. He is required also to make a report to the Legislature, concerning the condition of the funds, the distribution of the revenues and the condition and wants of the schools of the State, together with such recommendations, in regard to the improvement of the system as he may deem desirable. It is his duty to cause ten thousand (10,000) copies of his report to be published and distributed. He is also required to publish and distribute a sufficient number of copies of the school laws of the State. He is *ex officio* trustee of the State Normal School, and the president of the State Board of Education.

The State Board of Education consists of the State Superintendent of Public Instruction, who is *ex officio* its president, the Governor, the presidents of the State University, Normal School, and Purdue University, and the superintendents of the largest three cities of the State. The Board meets quarterly, and forms an advisory council of the State Superintendent. It issues instructions to county superintendents, and prepares printed lists of questions which are sent out to the county superintendents monthly and by them are submitted to the teachers who apply for licenses. The State Board is also empowered to grant State licenses to teachers of high character and standing which are valid for life. These examinations are conducted annually at various points in the State. The Board takes cognizance of such other educational matters as may properly come before it, and makes such recommendations to subordinate officers and to the Legislature as it may deem advisable. It appoints the trustees of the State University and the official visitors of the Normal School.

THE COUNTY SUPERINTENDENT is appointed by the board of County Commissioners biennially in June. He must be a citizen of the county in which he is appointed, and must have had two years successful experience as a teacher. It is his duty to examine applicants for license to teach in the branches required by law, and in such other branches as may be required by the voters at school meetings, or by school-boards of towns and cities. He licenses such as are found competent for six, twelve, eighteen, or twenty-four months, and receives a fee of one dollar from each applicant. He is required to visit and inspect all the schools of his county, at least once in each year, except those of cities employing a superintendent. The County Superintendent is required to hear and determine appeals from the decisions of the township trustees in relation to the employment, dismissal, and removal of a teacher; the renting, removal, or building of a school-house; and in relation to school meetings and the transactions thereof. In all local questions, the decision of the County Superintendent is final, although it does not abridge the right of any court of competent jurisdiction to take cognizance of such cases as might otherwise come before it. He receives statistical and financial reports from the trustees, and tabulates and transmits the same to the State Superintendent. He is authorized to revoke the license of a teacher who proves to be immoral or incompetent, or who neglects his business. He is required to hold a County Institute at least once each year, and to preside over a Township Institute at least once each month. He executes the orders of the State Board of Education, and transmits such information to the State Superintendent as may be required. He is president of the County Board of Education.

CITY AND TOWN TRUSTEES.—There may be three distinct municipal corporations in a county; the township, which is ordinarily six miles square, the incorporated town, and the city. The Board of School Trustees for a city or a town is composed of three members, one member retiring annually in June. The School Trustees in cities are appointed by the Common Council, and the School Trustees in towns by the Board of Town Trustees. 1. Such School Boards take general charge of the schools of their respective corporations; receive, pay out, and account for school moneys; build or otherwise provide school-houses; supply the schools with furniture, apparatus, etc.; employ teachers; and make rules and regulations for the government of the schools. They are required to make financial reports to the County Commissioners and certain financial and statistical reports to the County Superintendent, and they have power to order that certain local school taxes be levied. It is also their duty to take the enumeration of the school population once each year. 2. They may grade the schools and prescribe text-books, and they may appoint a superintendent and prescribe his duties. The School Board of the city of Indianapolis is organized under the provisions of a special act, and consists of eleven School Commissioners who are elected for three years by the people at a special election in June. They perform all the duties of City and Town Trustees, as stated above, and, in addition, have some special powers in the matter of levying taxes.

TOWNSHIP TRUSTEES.—Each township has a civil trustee, who is elected by the qualified voters of the township at a general election for a term of two years. The Civil Trustees are made by law the School Trustees for their respective townships. They perform the duties described in paragraph marked 1, under the preceding head. The Township Trustee, however, may be restricted in his powers by the action of the people. Each township has an average of nine districts. Tax-payers of a school district hold school meetings and elect a director. Such meetings may petition the trustee in regard to the building, repairing, or removal of a school-house, and they may also request the trustee to dismiss a teacher for just cause. The trustee can not employ any teacher whom a majority of those entitled to vote at school meetings have decided they do not wish employed.

Township Trustees must hold, or cause to be held, monthly township institutes for the instruction of the teachers. They may establish graded schools, or such modifications of them as may be practicable, and provide for the admission of such pupils, from the primary schools of the township, as are sufficiently advanced to enter them. The School Trustees of two or more distinct municipal corporations have power to establish joint graded schools or such modifications of them as may be practicable, and provide for the admission of such pupils of the primary schools of their corporations as are sufficiently advanced to enter them. A director presides at school meetings, visits schools, and, as agent of the trustee, takes charge of the school-house, provides fuel, and makes all temporary repairs.

The County Board of Education.—The County Board of Education consists of the Township Trustees and the School Trustees of towns and cities. It meets semi-annually in May and September. A majority of the trustees constitutes a quorum. This board considers the wants and needs of the schools and school property under its charge, and also all matters relating to the change and purchase of school furniture, books, maps, charts, etc. It may adopt text-books for towns and townships, and no text-book can be changed within three years from the date of its adoption, except by unanimous vote of all the members of the board.

School Funds.—The permanent school funds are divided into two classes:

1st. The Common School Fund, the sources of which are enumerated in the constitutional provisions previously quoted. The consolidated fund now amounts to nearly six and a half millions of dollars. Of this sum, the State has borrowed nearly four millions of dollars, for which she has given non-negotiable bonds bearing six per cent interest, payable semi-annually. The remainder of this amount has been apportioned to the counties, and has been loaned by the county auditors to individuals upon real estate mortgages at 8 per cent interest.

2d. The Congressional Township Fund, which is derived from the sale of the sixteenth section in each township, set apart to the townships by Congress for school purposes. This fund amounts to nearly two and a half millions of dollars, and is loaned by the county officers to individuals upon real estate mortgages at 8 per cent. The interest on these two funds is annually expended for tuition purposes only.

SCHOOL REVENUES.—The school revenues annually expended for tuition and other purposes are derived as follows:

1. The common school revenue for tuition consists chiefly of the proceeds of a state tax of sixteen cents on each one hundred dollars and fifty cents on each taxable poll, and the interest on the common school fund. This revenue is reported to the State Superintendent of Public Instruction by the proper authorities, and is paid into the State treasury, the State paying its interest on the non-negotiable bonds semi-annually; and the counties paying over the interest and the proceeds of the State tax which is due from them. This revenue is then apportioned semi-annually, in May and January, by the State Superintendent of Public Instruction to the various counties of the State, in proportion to the number of children of school age enumerated in each. The amount thus distributed last year was nearly two millions of dollars, being about three dollars *per capita* upon the enrollment.

2. The proceeds of the Congressional Township Fund are distributed by the county authorities to the congressional townships in proportion to that part of the fund owned by each respectively.

3. Trustees of townships, and the boards of school trustees in towns and cities, can each order a local levy in their respective corporations, not to exceed fifty cents on each one hundred dollars, and one dollar on each poll, in any one year. The sum arising from this tax is denominated Special School Revenue, and must be used for the construction, renting, or repairing of school-houses, providing furniture, school apparatus, and fuel therefor, and for the payment of other necessary expenses of the school except tuition.

4. The civil trustees of towns, and the common councils of cities, may, upon the petition of the school trustees of the respective corporations, levy an annual local tuition tax not exceeding twenty-five cents on each one hundred dollars of taxable property, and twenty-five cents on each taxable poll. This tax can also be levied by township trustees.

5. The board of civil trustees of a town, and the common councils of cities, may, upon petition of the school trustees thereof, issue the bonds of their respective corporations to an amount not exceeding in the aggregate fifty thousand dollars, payable in not less than one year nor more than twenty years after issuance, for the purpose of providing means to pay debts contracted by school trustees in the purchase of grounds or in the erection of school buildings. The civil authorities who may issue said bonds are required to levy an annual special tax not to exceed fifty cents on each one hundred dollars of taxable property, and

one dollar on each poll, for the purpose of paying the principal and interest of said bonds as they shall become due.

The total amount of tax possible in cities and towns, in any one year, under the law, is as follows, viz:

State tax on each $100	$.16;	on each poll	$ .50
Local tuition tax on each $100	.25;	" " "	.50
Local special tax	.50;	" " "	1.00
Special bond tax	.50;	" " "	1.00
Total	$1.41;	" " "	$3.00

In townships the limit is on property, $.91; on polls, $2.00.

6. The school board of Indianapolis can, in addition to the taxes mentioned above, make a levy of twenty-five cents on each one hundred dollars of taxable property for tuition purposes, and twenty-five cents on each one hundred dollars for building purposes, etc. It can also levy a tax of two cents on each one hundred dollars for free library purposes. The board is also authorized to issue bonds to the amount of one hundred thousand dollars in anticipation of the tax for building purposes.

Miscellaneous Provisions.—1. The teachers are required to make a report in writing, at the close of the school term, to the trustees, embracing a variety of statistical information concerning the schools. Until such a report is filed with the trustee, he is not allowed to pay the teacher more than 75 per cent of his wages.

2. Teachers are required to attend the sessions of the Township Institutes. These institutes must be held at least once each month and may be held, at the

discretion of the trustee, every two weeks. In case teachers are absent from these meetings, for any other cause than sickness, they forfeit one day's pay for every day's absence therefrom.

3. The common schools of a county are required to be closed during the session of the County Institute. This meeting is held at least once each year. The teachers are expected to be present, although there is no penalty for non-attendance.

4. Whenever the County Superintendent certifies to the County Auditor that an institute has been attended by at least twenty-five teachers, or persons preparing to become such, he is authorized to draw from the county treasury the sum of thirty-five dollars, to pay the expenses of the institute; and when the County Superintendent certifies that forty teachers, or persons preparing to become such, have attended the institute, fifty dollars can be drawn from the county treasury to pay the expenses.

5. Parents or guardians of school children can, with the consent of the Township Trustee and upon showing good cause, become detached from one school district in a township and be attached to another district. When persons living in one township can be better accommodated with school privileges in a school in an adjoining corporation, they may be transferred to the desired school by the trustee of the township in which they live. This transfer is for school purposes only.

6. An act approved May 31, 1869, after providing for the taxation of the property of colored persons for school purposes and for the enumeration of the colored children, reads as follows:

"The Trustee or Trustees of each township, town or city, shall organize the colored children into separate schools, having all the rights and privileges of other schools of the township: *Provided*, There are not a sufficient number within attending distance, the several districts may be consolidated and form one district. But if there are not a sufficient number within reasonable distance to be thus consolidated, the Trustee or Trustees shall provide such other means of education for said children as shall use their proportion, according to numbers, of school revenue to the best advantage;" and that "All laws relative to school matters, not inconsistent with this act, shall be deemed applicable to colored schools."

7. Section 147 reads as follows:

"The common schools of the State shall be taught in the English language, and the Trustee shall provide to have taught in them orthography, reading, writing, arithmetic, geography, English grammar, physiology, history of the United States, and good behavior, and such other branches of learning and other languages, as the advancement of pupils may require and the Trustee from time to time direct; and whenever the parents or guardians of twenty-five or more children in attendance at any school of a township, town or city, shall so demand, it shall be the duty of the School Trustee or Trustees of said township, town or city, to procure efficient teachers, and introduce the German language, as a branch of study, into such schools; and the tuition in said schools shall be without charge: *Provided*, such demand is made before the teacher for said district is employed."

8. Section 167 reads as follows:

"The Bible shall not be excluded from the public schools of the State."

STATISTICAL EXHIBIT.

1875.

I. ENUMERATION.

Number of white males . .	340,514	
Number of white females . .	317,434	
Total number of white children		657,948
Number of colored males . .	4,940	
Number of colored females . .	4,848	
Total number of colored children		9,788
Total enumeration . .		667,736
Number enumerated last year .		654,364
Increase		13,372

The increase in school population during the past seven years has been as follows, viz:

Enumeration of 1868	592,865
Increase for year ending September 1, 1869 .	17,699
Increase for year ending September 1, 1870 .	9,063
Increase for year ending September 1, 1871 .	3,101
Increase for year ending September 1, 1872 . .	8,811
Increase for eight months ending May 1, 1873	8,903
Increase for year ending May 1, 1874 . .	13,922
Increase for year ending May 1, 1875 . .	13,372
Total as above	667,736

ILLITERACY.—By reference to the United States census of 1870, it appears that there were in the State of Indiana, at that time, 26,783 children between the ages of 10 and 21 who could neither read nor write. After patient and careful inquiry, it was thought that the number of illiterate children was much smaller than was shown by this statement. Having all the machinery necessary for taking an accurate census of the school population, it was determined to make a separate enumeration of all illiterates between the ages of 10 and 21. This was done at the time of taking the last enumeration. In *seventy-nine* counties of the State, the reports show that there were but 4,234 illiterate children between the ages of 10 and 21. Upon the supposition that the counties that did not report, contain the same proportion of illiterates as the other counties, the total number of illiterates in the State would be 4,922.

While it is probable that a large share of those reported as illiterates by the United States Census in 1870 have now become of age and are therefore not included in the report taken by our school officers, a careful analysis of the facts will show one of two things to be true—that the census did us great injustice, or that our teachers have been doing some good work during the past five years.

II. School Attendance.

Number of white males enrolled in the schools	264,041	
Number of white females enrolled in the schools	231,670	
Total number of white children enrolled		495,711
Number of colored males enrolled in the schools	3,422	

Amount brought forward		495,711
Number of colored females enrolled in the schools	3,229	
Total number of colored children enrolled . . .		6,651
Total number of children enrolled in the schools during the year ending September 1, 1875		502,362

A careful inspection of the returns from several hundred school corporations shows that about 28 per cent of all children enumerated, and 15 per cent of all children enrolled, in the schools are over 15 years of age. Taking this with other quite reliable data, we construct the following interesting table:

Number of children enumerated under 15 years of age . . .		480,770
Number enrolled in public schools under 15 years of age . .	427,008	
Number enrolled in private schools (estimated)	30,000	
Total number between 6 and 15 receiving scholastic training		457,008
Number not in school last year		23,762

Thus it appears that 95 per cent of our school population between the ages of 6 and 15 received some scholastic training last year.

III. Additions to the School Funds.

1. *Common School Fund.*

Amount of fund held by counties in June, 1874		$2,408,393 04
Amount since added from fines by Clerks . .	$25,422 58	
Amount since added from fines by Justices . .	20,916 47	
Amount since added from other sources . .	3,675 72	
Total increase . .		50,014 77
Total amount held by counties June, 1875 . .		$2,458,407 81

2. *Congressional Township School Fund.*

Amount held by counties, June, 1874 .	$2,295,778 66
Amount since added, by sale of lands, etc.	35,044 71
Amount held by counties, June, 1875	$2,330,823 37
Value of 11,567 acres of unsold lands	105,177 25
Total Congressional Township School Fund	$2,436,000 62
Increase in Congressional Township School Fund for the year . .	$37,928 56

3. *Summary of School Funds.*

Common School Fund held by counties June, 1875 .	$2,458,407 81	
Non-negotiable bonds .	3,904,783 21	
Total Common School Fund . . .		$6,363,191 02
Congressional Township School Fund . .		2,436,000 62
Grand total . .		$8,799,191 64
Total amount held in June, 1874		8,711,248 31
Increase for the year		$87,943 33

IV. School Revenues.

Amount derived from State tax for the year ending November 1, 1875	$1,577,533 18	
Amount derived from interest on Common School Fund, held by counties, to November 15, 1875	192,271 52	
State's interest on non-negotiable bonds . .	234,287 00	
Amount derived from unclaimed fees, etc. .	3,200 85	
Total amount . .		$2,007,292 55

Amount brought forward	$2,007,292 55
Add amount of Congressional Township School Revenue reported by County Auditors	181,159 80
Add amount of local tuition tax collected to November 15, 1875, (estimated)	768,528 92
Add amount of proceeds of liquor licenses reported to this office to date .	202,365 00
Total amount of Tuition Revenue to November 15, 1875 . .	$3,159,346 27

This amount of tuition revenue is applicable to school purposes for the current school year ending June 30, 1876, and not for the year ending November 15, 1875.

Table Exhibiting the Growth

of the system as to various particulars, during the past twenty years, by semi-decades.

YEAR.	*Length of School in Days.*	*Number of Teachers.*	*Attendance at School.*	*Total Amount Paid Teachers.*
1855.	61	4,016	206,994	$239,924
1860.	65	7,649	303,744	481,020
1865.	66	9,493	402,812	1,020,440
1870.	97	11,826	462,527	1,810,866
1875.	130	13,133	502,362	2,830,747

MISCELLANEOUS STATISTICS.

1875.

School days in year	130
County Superintendents	92
City Systems	40
Town Systems	202
District Graded-Schools	396
Ungraded Schools	8,940
School Corporations	1,253
School Officers	1,845
School-houses	9,307
Number of Teachers	13,133
County Institutes	91
Attendance at same	11,103
Number of Township Institutes	4,080
Houses erected during year	382
Enumeration of Children	667,736
Enrollment in Schools	502,362
School Fund	$8,799,191
Additions to Fund during year	$87,943
Value of School Property	$10,870,338

REVENUE FOR THE YEAR.

From Liquor Licenses, etc.	$205,565
Interest on Fund	607,718
State Tax	1,577,533
Local Tax	2,650,623
Total	$5,041,439

SOURCES OF TUITION REVENUE.

The following table shows the resources of our Tuition Revenues, and the amounts of the same for each year from 1866 to the present time.

Years.	Taxes.	Interest on Common Fund.	Liquor Licenses.	Unclaimed Fees.	State's Indebtedness Paid.	Interest Paid by State on Bonds.	Interest on Congressional Fund.	Amounts of Delinquencies.	Local Tuition Taxes as Distributed by County Auditors.	Total.
1866	$910585 37	$111425 32	$84225 00	$1584 59	$50090 00		$150043 57	$24000 00		$1330863 79
1867	937842 87	98885 36	76500 00	1286 38	40573 56	$150826 73				....
1868	864548 01	97629 07	80000 00	1038 02	50000 00	202024 92	154036 92	117227 74		1566507 58
1869	987563 41	108710 38	89258 00	1249 75	50000 00	213024 97	154447 33	23864 71		1628172 56
1870	1012357 74	101814 65	81700 00	451 01	50000 00	213078 96	146548 86	91586 01		1697537 23
1871	1051438 57	112650 23	99809 17	985 46		223740 96	144781 06	35750 00		1669155 45
1872	1070301 69	160840 10	108280 00	500 38		223740 96	146980 21	6800 00		1717243 34
1873	1190626 65	189455 47	40212 50	7193 72		234064 50	98988 12	27382 86	$530667 80	2276569 75
1874	1013463 42	173542 19	35000 00	8438 09		234287 00	172209 82	63516 87	551785 74	2211328 13
1875	1577533 18	192271 52	202365 00	3200 85		234287 00	181159 80		768528 92	3159346 27

Number and Value of School-Houses.

Number and kind of school-houses, and valuation of school property in each year during the last decade.

Year.	Stone.	Brick.	Frame.	Log	Total.	Total Valuation.
1866	78	566	6145	1096	8231	$4,515,734 00
1867	71	554	6672	1063	8360	5,078,356 00
1868	74	592	9906	831	8403	5,828,501 00
1869	76	655	7207	723	8661	6,577,258 33
1870	83	725	7436	583	8327	7,282,639 30
1871	85	834	7517	513	8949	7,381,839 73
1872	88	877	7568	547	9080	9,199,480 00
1873	87	960	7797	458	9302	9,404,039 70
1874	82	1117	7657	279	9129	10,373,692 58
1875	92	1235	7753	227	9307	10,870,338 18

School-Houses Erected.

The statement of the number and cost of school-houses erected during the last decade is as follows:

Year.	Number.	Cost.	Average Cost.
1866	346	No report.	
1867	364	No report.	
1868	424	$587,563 49	$1385
1869	405	556,607 00	1374
1870	498	653,189 22	1311
1871	415	609,105 67	1467
1872	393	561,813 55	1429
1873	465	872,900 73	1877
1874	499	875,515 33	1754
1875	382	649,145 14	1699

Tabular View of System.

Officers.

Superintendent Public Instruction.
State Board of Education.
County Superintendents.
City and Town Trustees.
Township Trustees.

Institutions General.

Ungraded Schools.
District Graded Schools.
Town and City Schools.

University System.

State University, Bloomington
Normal School, Terre Haute.
Purdue University, (Industrial) Lafayette.

Institutions Charitable.

School for the Blind, Indianapolis.
School for Deaf Mutes, Indianapolis.
Soldiers' Orphans' Home, Knightstown.

Institutions Reformatory.

Boys' Reformatory, Plainfield.
Girls' Reformatory, Indianapolis.

Institutions Special.

County and Township Institutes, Compulsory.
State Teachers' Association, Voluntary.

School Age, between 6 and 21.
Attendance, voluntary.

STATISTICS RELATING TO

NAME OF INSTITUTION.	LOCATION.	Year of its Organization.
St. Meinard, College and Seminary	St. Meinard	1861
Smithson College	Logansport	1872
Concordia College	Ft. Wayne	1839
Ft. Wayne College	Ft. Wayne	1846
Spiceland Academy	Spiceland	1872
Earlham College	Richmond	1859
Friends Academy	Richmond	1869
Collegiate Institute	La Grange	1839
Indiana State University	Bloomington	1824
Hanover College	Hanover	1828
Union Christian College	Merom	1859
St. Michael's Academy	Plymouth	1870
Collegiate Institute	Battle Ground	1857
Collegiate Institute	Stockwell	1860
Seminary	Green Hill	1869
Male and Female College	Bedford	1871
Moravian Female Seminary	Hope	1868
Hartsville University	Hartsville	1859
St. Bonaventure's College	Terre Haute	1872
St. Joseph's Academy	Terre Haute	1872
Commercial College	Terre Haute	1862
Oxford Academy	Oxford	1866
Moore's Hill College	Moore's Hill	1854
Aged Poor's Home	Indianapolis	1873
Bloomingdale Academy	Bloomingdale	1846
Green Hill Academy	Columbia City	1873
Franklin College	Franklin	1844
Wabash College	Crawfordsville	1833
Indiana Asbury University	Greencastle	1837
Female College	Greencastle	1870
Vincennes University	Vincennes	1838
De Pauw College	New Albany	1845
N. W. C. University	Indianapolis	1852
University of Notre Dame	Notre Dame	1842
St. Mary's Academy	Notre Dame	1855
St. Joseph's Academy	South Bend	1865
Totals	36	

HIGHER INSTITUTIONS, 1874.

Number of Faculty.	Total Number of Students.	Total Number of Alumni.	Number of volumes in Library.	Amount of Endowment.	Value of Building, Grounds, Furniture, Apparatus, and Libraries.
	62				
6	115		500	$12,500	$101,000
	252		5000		150,250
10	112		500		80,250
6	445	31	2000	3,000	13,300
11	233	76	3700	57,000	157,500
6	130	12			25,250
4	149			10,000	7,000
26	392	987	8000	110,000	190,000
11	124	404	7000	130,000	145,000
3	156	11		100,000	800
5					12,000
4	240	11	1500	25,000	41,200
6	239	20	100		20,500
2	68			12,000	12,000
5	115		30	15,000	2,000
8	64	29	500		31,000
7		32			12,000
7	155		600		31,500
	135				
4	300				4,000
5	241				7,075
5	164	79	400	18,000	31,000
7	33		50		
4	157		1000		11,300
2	61				1,500
4	50	38	1000	50,000	40,000
11	217	273	1300	160,000	172,500
8	458	500	8000	165,000	203,300
6	130				20,000
3	65	4	400	41,500	8,100
7	92	91	1000		51,500
11	153	123	1500	250,000	303,500
38	503	100	1000		221,000
40	266	13	7000		195,000
9	160	2	700		45,500
291	6236	2836	52780	$1,159,000	$2,347,825

INDEX.

INDEX.

(*The numbers refer to pages.*)

www.ingramcontent.com/pod-product-compliance
Lightning Source LLC
LaVergne TN
LVHW050521100826
845148LV00002B/405